RAISING MEAT GOATS IN A COMMERCIAL OPERATION

IN THE MIDWEST

GREG CHRISTIANSEN

ISBN: 0615584128

ISBN-13: 9780615584126

ENDORSEMENTS

This book is just what the goat industry needs if it is ever going to make the leap from being a backyard hobby operation to becoming a legitimate food animal production industry. While there are many books about raising meat goats available, this one is different in that it is the only book that addresses how to manage meat goats on a commercial scale. Author Greg Christiansen draws on his years of experience in raising meat goats on a commercial scale to explain the principles of managing meat goats as a viable farm business. Greg tells you how to breed does that are capable of working for you and the necessary management to enable the does to do their job. He has excellent sections on fencing goats, working facilities for goats, protecting goats from predators, wintering goats and many other subjects necessary for raising meat goats. This is the most practical how-to book with real life examples of making management decisions to solve problems I've seen. For the producer seeking to raise goats on a commercial scale, this is the only book available with the necessary information and it will be the best money you ever invested in your goat business.

Dr. Steve Hart
Goat Extension Specialist
Langston University
Langston, OK.

Meat goats are the fastest growing livestock type in the U.S. today, but too many new breeders fail to recognize the differences between raising show goats and commercial goat production. Ten years ago not much was known about what would work best for commercial production and early breeders had to learn through trial and error. Greg Christiansen has made his experience available to help you avoid the pitfalls most new commercial breeders must navigate.

Dr. David Sparks DVM
Oklahoma State University
Cooperative Extension Service

Greg's Book is an easy read and should be required for anyone looking to get into commercial meat goat production in a big way. As Greg discovered early on, experience with cattle does not always translate to successful management of goats. Through trial, error, ingenuity and persistence, he has transformed his goat operation into a key component that blends well with his cattle and row crop enterprises. Success with meat goats often takes hard work, but this book offers advice, tips and insights that make the job easier from Day 1. I highly recommend it.

Terry Hankins
Egypt Creek Ranch
Publisher/Editor *Goat Rancher Magazine*

As the largest goat producer in Kansas, Greg Christiansen has the credibility to write and publish a book on raising pasture meat goats.

I have known Greg for more than 25 years and have seen him apply a logical systems approach to many enterprises. He demands efficiency from all input factors- plant, animal, human and machinery. I have seen Greg's meat goat operation in person, and can testify that his goats live in an environment that requires them to work for a living. His goats live more like their ancestors from hundreds of years ago than their contemporaries of today.

I have read, Raising Meat Goats In A Commercial Operation, and can recommend it to anyone who has goats, wants goats, or someone who thinks they might someday be interested in getting in the goat business.

Johnny Wade Gaspard
Master of Agribusiness Management
Livestock Consultant

I read and then reread this book and I think it's great. I liked the style. It was pretty much like the day we came out to ride around and check goats with Greg. It was easy to read and covered a lot of information you can't find anywhere else.

I really like the honest, open style of the book. I liked the photos of the working chute and especially of the dog feeding enclosure. That was one of the things we really liked when we visited your place. I think the information on goat browsing, feeding and nutrition was really good. I also got a great deal of information about taking care of the kids once they hit the ground. No one else I'm aware of talks about these issues or even about working goats on a large scale. This is where I think the book will really pay off to the people who purchase and read it.

This kind of book just can't be found anywhere I know of, and I've looked pretty hard.

Erin Snider,
Pasture Meat Goat Producer expanding to
several hundred does in the future.

I think this is a great book. It's one of a kind. I've read several other goat books, but none that go into such detail and covers the business of managing commercial meat goats. It's very easy to read and you won't want to put it down. I enjoyed it very much and would recommend it to anyone who has or would like to start a commercial goat herd. This book talks about goats in a whole different perspective and shows that you can successfully raise goats on a large scale pasture operation. It's great that this book was written by the rancher himself with firsthand experience.

Rob Wood
Middlecreek Meat Goats

As someone with a livestock background but limited goat experience, I can read this book and get an honest understandable perspective from someone who is actually making it work in the Midwest. The question and answer approach makes this a great reference for real life problems that will most definitely occur in this business. Anyone who is or plans to raise commercial goats, especially in our region NEEDS this book.

Brian Lueker
County Executive Director
Linn County Kansas
Farm Service Agency

Greg is a wealth of knowledge for commercial goats. What he speaks is honest and true for our area of the country. I know, for I have suffered and appreciated many of the issues he has covered here. Thank you for writing this must read book.

Scott Hobson
Once a Backyard goat producer,
now a Pasture goat producer.

After reading Greg's book I found it to be a must have for the serious goat producer. If you purchase this book and read it and apply it's practices toward your new or existing operation, you will potentially save yourself time, money and heartache in your own pasture meat goat endeavors.

Shane Deering
Manager St. Joseph, Missouri
Sheep and Goat Auction

DEDICATION

Any profit made from sales of this book will go toward reaching people with the gospel of Jesus Christ. That may be my neighbor down the road, or yours, or someone several continents away or in-between or maybe even you.

CONTENTS

ABOUT THE AUTHOR

After receiving a Bachelor of Science degree from Kansas State University in Animal Science, Greg made his living for several years on cattle ranches to feedlots from Colorado, Missouri, Texas and Oklahoma. He then moved with his wife, Ann, son Tanner and two daughters, Megan and Ashley, to a farm in east central Kansas and began a row crop farming and cattle operation. About 12 years ago he started buying meat goats and began to grow his herd with the occasional help of his son Tanner. In a typical year, Greg will have more than 600 commercial does kidding, along with raising corn, soybeans wheat, hay and cattle.

INTRODUCTION

(I NEVER READ THESE EITHER,
BUT PLEASE READ THIS ONE.)

Will this book be worth your money and time?

I know that typically people put something in the introduction that makes people want to read the book. You would have someone well known write it so that they could tell others how great the book is and how it will help them. At the very least the writer would write something in the introduction that makes people want to read it. After reading what I just wrote I'm not sure I did that…no, I'm sure I haven't.

I don't want you to waste any of your valuable time or money, so before you read through several chapters of this book you may want to decide if this is the kind of book from which you would benefit. I will now tell you who this book isn't for and what you won't learn from it. I am sure this will greatly limit the audience but at least those who read it will get what they paid for.

This is not a beginner's book for someone who has no livestock experience at all and wants to start raising meat goats. Personally, if you don't have any previous livestock experience, I would recommend starting with something besides goats or at least start out with only a few head. There are many other books written for backyard type goat producers that you should consult before reading this book. I am assuming that the reader has some personal experience and a general knowledge of livestock production.

Within this book you will not find out how to groom, show or judge show goats.

You won't see pictures of various goat breeds and where they originated.

You won't find recipes for cooking goat meat, making goat soap, or goat cheese, or learn how to pasteurize goat milk.

I'm not going to tell you how to teach a goat to pull a cart.

Those things are not included in this book because there are other people who are experts in those areas. If you would like information in those areas you should buy a book from them.

You won't find symptoms and diagnosis of all the diseases that goats can get and the medical treatments for each. This is not a goat veterinarian handbook. There are not many drugs labeled for goats, so it is unlawful and unethical for me or anyone besides a veterinarian to suggest a treatment for a disease or goat problem involving most antibiotic treatments. A good book you should get for that information is "Sheep & Goat Medicine" by D.G. Pugh and consult a veterinarian.

I wrote this for those who are familiar with handling and raising other livestock and want to integrate commercial meat goats into their current business, or those who have been raising goats and would like to expand but don't quite know how to overcome the obstacles they've encountered so far.

More specifically I wrote for those in the Midwest United States, eastward to the Atlantic ocean. If you look at a map of the U.S. and make a dot about a hundred miles west of Minnesota, and another one a hundred miles west of Louisiana, and connect the dots drawing a line north and south and went east from there to the Atlantic Ocean, the pasture conditions are very similar. Pastures are smaller in size, rainfall is greater and the weeds and brush take over pastures at a faster rate than anywhere I've been west of that line. Our problems and management style will be drastically different from those in western Kansas, West Texas, Wyoming, and Montana, Arizona or other Western states.

If you are a registered breeding stock producer, I would recommend that you read this book to understand your potential customer better and be able to raise breeding stock that will meet the needs of the commercial producer. It doesn't seem to me that the registered goat producer knows much about the commercial producer and the problems he faces in making a profit raising meat goats and selling them on the commercial market. I have had only one producer of breeding stock come to my place and look at how I produced goats and what kind of bucks I would like to see breeding my does and what type of does I needed to raise kids in my environment and management system. You can spend a lot of money raising registered breeding stock but eventually those bucks must make the commercial producer money if you're going to sell them to him.

So, if you are familiar with livestock and may want to raise meat goats and maybe raise a lot of them as a business — not a hobby — you are the person for whom I have written down these things.

Every year there are a few people who want to get into the goat business or have some goats but want to expand and treat them more like cattle on pasture. Some will come and ride in the pickup with me as I am feeding or checking goats. They are interested in how goats are raised in a larger, less confined way than what they have seen or been doing up until that time. As they ride along and open gates or tag kids or help catch a doe having one issue or another, they will ask questions ranging from kidding, weaning, deworming, marketing goats, fencing and livestock guardian dogs. After we have checked several pastures and several hundred goats, they are ready to leave and have forgotten half of what we talked about simply due to sensory overload.

I have been asked if there is a book I would recommend for raising pasture goats. After looking for a book about commercial goat production and finding the selection very slim, I decided to attempt one myself.

There are many books about raising goats but I have not found one that is written by someone who raises large herds of commercial goats in pasture situations, where they are treated more like cattle than like pets or 4-H projects. I don't mind talking to people and answering their questions about goats, but I have discovered some people feel like they are intruding and would more readily consult a book.

This book is different from any other book I have found about raising goats in that it is written by someone who is raising commercial goats on a large scale — from kidding until they are sold as finished meat goats.

The Eastern half of the United States is not traditionally meat goat country and it is uncharted territory for raising them on open range or pasture situations. But this is where I live; it is what I have to work with, and the Eastern part of the U.S. is where the most recent growth in meat goats is taking place. It is also where there is the most potential for future growth in the industry.

In this book, Raising Meat Goats In A Commercial Operation, I will mostly be explaining what we do and why we do it that way. I believe raising meat goats is half skill and the other half art, "Skart".

What I describe in the following pages is not always the text book way, it is not the only way, but it is considered by me at this time to be the most efficient and practical way for me to handle goats and their issues and be profitable in Eastern Kansas where we live. If you are going to raise enough goats to be profitable or have other ongoing enterprises, you will have many demands on your time and resources. For me, this means that on any given day I may need to be planting or combining corn or soybeans, spraying our fields or working cattle. Every minute has more than one job waiting to be done.

Labor is a valuable commodity so corners begin to get cut and things put off until later or sometimes never. This is simply what we do and what works for us, (my son, Tanner, when he can help, and myself) at this time. We may change some things as we become more efficient or discover new information or a better way of doing something from other producers. I rarely come away from visiting another goat operation that I don't get a new idea I can use or adapt to our situation.

When my son and I were starting into meat goat production and looking for large goat producers to visit in our general climate area, there simply were not any. That is mostly still the case today. We made many mistakes and had several problems. Most people probably would have given up and gotten out of the goat business. Maybe that is why we didn't find any large operations to visit. It has taken several years and literally hundreds of mistakes that cost us a great deal in time and money to get a herd that is more easily managed.

Our goal was to be able to raise goats much like cattle are raised. They should be able to take care of themselves for the most part, needing assistance only occasionally. As long as they have feed and water they should be mostly trouble free. That is what we thought raising goats would be like when we got goats more than 10 years ago. But that has only been the case in the last few years.

So get in the pickup and ride along as I try to anticipate questions you'll ask and answer them with practical experience. But don't get too comfortable, you'll be opening the gates and we have 8 to 10 pastures to stop at with 60 to over 100 does in each pasture.

CHAPTER 1

PASTURE GOATS OR BACKYARD GOATS?

After several years raising meat goats, I've come to find out there are two types of goats, backyard goats and pasture goats.

Backyard goats are produced in small quantities in small lots or maybe 10- to 20-acre small pastures. They are usually hand fed ample amounts of feed supplements and have adequate shelter. Their toes are neatly trimmed. Most of their owners think they are very cute and give them names. These are not bad things and backyard goats will thrive in these backyard conditions. They will wean very large kids and probably get a ribbon at the fair.

By contrast, pasture goats, as the name implies, will spend their lives in larger pastures ranging up to several hundred acres. They will be bred and kid in range conditions using brush and trees that they haven't eaten for shelter. They will be given only the amount of feed necessary to provide adequate and economical nutritional supplementation to their forage-based range diet. They may grow long toes and might never see a pair of hoof trimmers. They may be called many names, none of which I will put in print. Pasture goats are not mismanaged goats or goats that are not well taken care of. They are raised for a different purpose by a different type of livestock producer with a different management philosophy.

I make this distinction because when my son, Tanner, and I were starting a goatherd from scratch, buying goats at sales and from individuals, we wanted to buy pasture goats. But most all of the goats that are raised in the Midwest are back-yard goats. That meant that most of the goats for sale were backyard goats. I'm not suggesting that they are inferior. They were fine goats for their previous owners and they did well in the environment in which they were raised and were accus-tomed to. When we purchased them, some had huge kids on them and were in great body condition.

So like the cattle that I had managed and had made a living caring for, I turned them out to pasture. But what I didn't know then is that there are two types of goats. And that is why I bring it up to you now, as obvious as it seems. But if you are a cattleman thinking about getting into goats, it will never cross your mind that there are two kinds of goats, backyard goats and pasture goats.

> *There are two kinds of goats, backyard goats and pasture goats.*

You may have to look hard to find females from herds that are being managed in the way you want to raise goats. You may have already begun your herd with backyard goats as we did. In that case you will have to breed the pasture survival techniques into them. This simply means that you get rid of the ones that don't produce or don't bring a kid home from the pasture. It also means that it is a bigger challenge to get a herd that is easy to manage and maintain. It can be done successfully but your perseverance and stamina will be tested.

How'd you get into goats?

My son and I started in the meat goat business in 2001. We had previously been through several very dry summers and all that would grow in the pastures was weeds and brush. I was meeting with Duff Sandness every week to teach me how to train my Border Collie to gather cattle. He starts the training on goats and said he would pick me up a few at a sale he was going to. They were to cost about $15 to $20 a head. The next week he told me he couldn't get any bought because they were higher than he had expected: $30 to $40 each for does and their kids were bringing $.65-$.75 a pound at the time. Being in the livestock business, I put some conservative cash flow numbers together.

All the research I looked at said to expect no more than 170% kid crop but that you could kid twice in three years and a doe should kid at 1 year old but may have only one kid that first year. The kids should weigh 60 lb. - 70 lb. when weaned at 4 months of age. Unfortunately, these numbers must have been taken from small backyard goat operations. I showed my numbers to Duff and we were both at the next sale getting started in the meat goat business, buying Boer and Boer cross nannies. Tanner and I took several trips looking at meat goat operations but we didn't come across any that were larger pasture operations. Maybe that should have told us something. After talking with mostly backyard goat owners I adjusted my kidding down to once a year and my kid crop percentage down to 150%. It still seemed profitable but I was naively over optimistic. After a couple discouraging years of less than 80% kid crops and labor-intensive kidding seasons due to the lack of mothering ability, Duff and I both sold our Boer bucks and got some Spanish bucks on a trip to south Texas.

Please don't think I am Boer bashing. They are fast growing, heavily muscled goats, and I wish I was a good enough manager to raise them by the hundreds in the climate of the Midwestern United States.

Duff soon went into the registered Kiko business and I stayed with the commercial goats using Spanish and Kiko bucks. As my homegrown replacement does began coming into the herd

I noticed that they were more productive, being better mothers to their kids with less parasite problems. I then made a costly mistake. Meat goats had gotten up to $1.00/lb. and many people were buying females. We were keeping most of our females and increasing our herd size very slowly. So I purchased 250 head of Boer-cross does from out of state for more than $100 a head. I did not understand the backyard goat concept yet but I would soon get a costly lesson. These does started kidding in a freak early April snowstorm. Needless to say, that didn't go well. Very few of those does are left on our place today due to lack of mothering ability. That is our No. 1 culling criteria. A doe that has a dry udder when I wean the kids will get a ride to town. If her bag is dry at weaning, that means she had lost her kid several weeks before or never had one.

Being too stubborn — or dumb — to sell out and quit the goat business, I kept at it, and about seven years into it I started to have better kidding seasons and more kids sold per nanny. I could see our home-raised does were the better mothers but since we had left the Boer influence, our selling weight and feed efficiency suffered. I am currently using larger Myotonic bucks and TexMasters, a cross of Myotonic and Boer, on my Kiko-type does to put some depth and width into the kids. I also still use some Kiko bucks. I really like those Kiko-cross mothers.

In my opinion, mothering ability and parasite resistance are the keys to overall profitability and is the result of selecting animals for several generations that are adapted to your environment and management and culling those that aren't.

It comes from raising generations of goats that become adapted to your environment and management, as a breed trait. That being said, there are

In my opinion, mothering ability and parasite resistance are the keys to overall profitability and is the result of selecting animals for several generations that are adapted to your environment and management and culling those that aren't.

some breeds that natural selection may try to put you out of business before you realize the benefits of it.

If you ask me what breed of goat a certain doe on our place is, I may not be able to tell you but the reason she is still here is maybe 30% due to her breeding and 70% due to the differences within the breed or her personal hardiness regardless of her breed. I believe you could take many breeds and make them pasture goats in your environment, but it will be more costly and take longer with some breeds.

Good bucks are important but the does are the ones who bring home the bacon.

When we first started buying goats to begin our goatherd, my thought was to buy medium quality nannies and then spend more money buying high quality bucks. That same strategy works well in the cattle business. The problem with this is that at the time 70 lb. kid goats were selling for $50-$60, nannies were selling for only $30-$50. So if one kid from that nanny would sell for more than the breeding stock cost, what type of nannies would someone be getting rid of at the local sale barn? It would only be one that wouldn't raise a kid. These are the type of nannies that I and several others were buying to start our goatherds. We were expecting to be able to breed them up in a few years using a quality Boer buck. The problem is that they were being sold because they were terrible mothers. Then they are dumped out in a pasture environment and expected to keep track of a couple kids.

The first few years we had goats, I would be out checking them during kidding season and find newborn kids that had not been licked off or nursed and no mother around. We had several bottle kids in the earlier years but our success rate with them was very limited. One year we had a late snow, 8" of heavy wet snow coming down in the heart of April kidding season, after several inches of rainfall the day before. I don't have to tell you how that one turned out.

Backyard does kidding in pasture situations with several days of 35-45 degree wet weather does not spell success. I would go out for hours and started picking up abandoned kids. They were lying in the mud and their moms had run under cedar trees to get out of the weather.

No matter how good your buck is, your does are the ones who are going to

> *Your does are the ones who are going to raise your kids and stick with them, standing over them with her legs spread like an umbrella, in a rain or hail storm.*

raise your kids and stick with them, standing over them with her legs spread like an umbrella, in a rain or hail storm. That is more valuable than any buck I ever bought. Is that a learned trait or a breed trait? I'm not sure but maybe it is that some breeds learn faster than others.

Looking back, one of the biggest mistakes we made when starting our goatherd was that we should have spent more money on the does, buying good pasture does from a producer in the same type climate and with similar management.

Granted, we didn't know anyone raising goats on pasture on a large scale at that time and even today I think it is rare in the Midwest. There are many larger goat operations in Texas but that is traditional goat country for a reason. Their climate is such that parasites are not as big of an issue to them. If you are in a higher rainfall and colder climate than West Texas, I would not recommend bringing goats from there to your climate and expect them to thrive.

After five years we probably didn't have more than 25 of those 250 goats left on the place. They have left in one way or another — mostly due to parasites and mothering ability. They were all sale barn does, coming from a backyard environment, being thrown into a pasture situation with parasites, predators and Midwestern springtime storms that they had not known.

> *We should have spent more money on the does, buying good pasture does from a producer in the same type climate and with similar management.*

Don't get me wrong, breeding to a good buck is very important. But many times when I went to look at and buy herd sires, the bucks that the producer was most proud of and wanted thousands of dollars for would all be in small dry-lot pens with self-feeders full of a specially formulated grain ration that he could also sell me. He would be telling me how this breed never has to be dewormed and how big and fast growing they are. I had my doubts if they had ever eaten a blade of grass with a parasite attached to it. He would show me their mothers that they had purchased for several thousand dollars more, that had spent their life in similar pens. Then he would proudly take me to his heated kidding barn, where all the does come to be put in individual pens to kid and claim their babies. These barns were really nice and I wished at the time I had something like it at home.

He might show me a pen of buck kids that were for sale from this year's kid crop. Maybe there would be 30 head in the pen. I've ask him how many does he has and he has already told me that he has 35 does and how they never lose many kids. I know by this information that he never culls any of the slow growing kids but that they are all here in the pen and the other pen that has about 30 head of weaned nanny kids in it, waiting for somebody to write a check. I would be picking out the top buckling from a herd of 30 head if I wanted to pay the price.

He tells me he usually sells out quickly and that I should at least give him a deposit on one or two now.

In an earlier conversation, we had talked about the local goat sales and he had been complaining that they never pay him the price per pound they should and he believes their scales to be wrong because his goats never weigh what he thinks they should. Now I know he takes some to the local auction market, maybe he doesn't sell out, and I know they are not considered #1 market goats bringing a premium or even average market price or he wouldn't feel cheated. So if I breed my does to one of these bucks, that, by his own admission, won't bring top or even average price per pound at the market that I work with, and don't weigh as much as they should, what should I expect?

I really can't fault these producers though. They are good marketers and have spent a lot of time promoting their product, and if I had goats worth that kind of money I wouldn't want to risk letting them out of their pens into an uncontrolled pasture environment either. They have probably made more money raising goats than I have. But I'm not sure it's because their goats are any better. Honestly, at the risk of sounding conceited and boastful, when I go to look at other goats, it makes me like mine more. Yours will be the same way too, trust me.

But if this is the way you want to raise goats then I would readily recommend you buy them from this type of breeder.

If you are expecting to raise pasture goats then don't do as I have done, spending a lot of money on big, pretty, backyard type bucks.

I have a friend who raises Myotonic and Myotonic X Boer goats. He lives only a few miles from me and has limited acreage, but his operation is definitely not a backyard type. I will try to buy a couple bucks from him every year and then keep some of my own top-growing buck kids. I think that if I have several hundred buck kids and there are three or four top individuals from that many kids, there is something that has made them better than their contemporaries in the same environment. It is usually parasite resistance, mothering ability and milk production of his dam, weaning weight, average daily gain and feed efficiency — all the things for which I select.

> *If you are expecting to raise pasture goats then don't do as I have done, spending a lot of money on big, pretty, backyard type bucks.*

CHAPTER 2

PARASITES, A GOAT'S ACHILLES HEEL

People often ask about my deworming schedule and how often we deworm. I don't deworm my goats until my goats need deworming. For several years they needed it often, maybe more often than we dewormed them due to time restraints imposed by other obligations common on any farm or ranch.

Now the does are all gathered in late February or early March and given a CDT vaccination, which prevents what is called, "over eating disease or enterotoxemia. This is caused by clostridium Perfringens type C and type D. It can be a problem when changes in diet occur or when feeding higher amounts of grain when getting the kids ready for market. This same vaccine can contain a Tetanus vaccination as well. A Pneumonia vaccine is also given at this time to help protect against many respiratory diseases. Colorado Serum is the only one I know of that has a Pneumonia vaccine labeled for goats. It is called, "Mannheimia Haemolytica Pasteurella Multocida Bacterin" and can be bought over the counter. You will probably need to order it as not many veterinarians may keep it in stock. Both of these vaccines need to be given twice the first year, about 2-3 weeks apart, then once annually. By revaccinating the does 1-2 months before they kid will help to protect the kids through the mother's antibodies that she passes through the colostrum. They are dewormed during this revaccination time.

My doe herd will start kidding in late March and are usually done by late April. After kidding, I want to be able leave them in the pastures they kid in, although I will move them to another paddock within a pasture if I have one. It is difficult to kid 50 - 100 does in a pasture and then load them and their kids in a trailer and move them to another pasture. Rounding up those kids is like herding cats; I've done it but I try to avoid it.

I prefer to not deworm them again until I wean the kids in late July or August. Not that they don't need it and not that it isn't a good practice to go ahead and check them and deworm the ones that need it. But due to the fact that in my business I am planting, spraying and harvesting crops for the farming operation and also baling hay, catching and deworming several hundred does and their kids doesn't usually get priority unless I am having problems with a particular pasture, as in dead goats.

I have had situations where I've had to gather and deworm a certain group of goats. If I have to move a group of does during the summer, or gather them for some other reason, I would go ahead and take that opportunity to deworm the ones that need it while I have them up. I'm not saying this is the best way but this is the way that it usually gets done here.

> *My does must be able to carry a worm load and still produce.*

My does must be able to carry a worm load and still produce. I am sure I have lost does by doing it this way and culled many out by natural selection, but however you manage your doe herd is how you will have to manage it in the future. If you have does you need to deworm every month of the summer, so you do, you will always have does that you have to deworm every month. My desire is to handle my goats as little as possible, only deworming when I am doing other things with them. I think this should be the goal of all goat producers. I think people with a small herd of goats enjoy handling them. They may believe they should deworm them on some type of regular schedule, so they do, therefore they continually have to.

How many goats can I run on an acre?

There are other ways that I try to limit the worm load that the goats have to live with. I usually stock a pasture with 1 to 1.5 goats per acre. I am in an area of 36" of rainfall a year so I usually have enough forage for a higher stocking rate, but the goats will not do as well and you will be deworming more often the closer they eat to the ground. I will oftentimes add some cattle, whatever the pasture will accommodate. They will help vacuum up the goat parasites and the goats will help mop up the cattle parasites. Parasitologists tell me that stomach worms are host specific and neither species is affected by the other's internal parasites. Of course it helps if the goats are eating brush because it is up off the ground and will usually not be infected. If you've had goats for more than a couple years, they probably have eaten most of the brush and are forced to eat more grass and broadleaves.

I have read that you can stock goats up to 4 or 5 head per acre. I have never seen that myself in a larger, continual goat operation. This might be a good way to quickly rid a pasture of brush for one season, but after that, if the goats did have enough forage they would eventually have more problems with that stocking rate. If you find someone stocking goats at that rate and they can deworm their goats only a couple times a year, I would buy goats from them. You will save yourself years of breeding for that type of goat. Personally, I have never found that person. Some may run 4 to 5 head per acre in small paddocks and rotate them through several pastures during the year. This is a good management practice for forage growth and to break the parasite cycle, but they are usually stocking at an overall rate of 1 to 2 head per acre, when it is all said and done. I do have some pastures split up so I can rotate them throughout the summer but very few and I simply don't have the man hours to get it done as intensely as it should be.

> *you should buy breeding stock from a goat rancher that is in your general climate area and who raises goats and manages them in a manner similar to what you are planning to do.*

I cannot stress enough that when a person begins to buy goats and start a goatherd you should buy breeding stock from a goat rancher that is in your general climate area and who raises goats and manages them in a manner similar to what you are planning to do. You may think that these goats cost too much and you could buy breeding stock cheaper somewhere else, but it will cost you much more in the long run and you will become very discouraged for several years. If you cannot afford to buy these types of goats, then you cannot afford to start into the goat business. If you cannot find a producer that is in your climate zone and handling goats the way you would do so in your future operation, you will be forced to start with goats that will not thrive in your management system. You need to be prepared for a few years of challenging goat production, but it can be done if you have the tenacity.

What dewormer should I use?

There are actually very few dewormers labeled for use in goats. You will need to have a working relationship with your veterinarian and have him prescribe a dewormer for you and give you the withdrawal time before slaughter for that dewormer.

I have been using a particular dewormer since we started in goats and have not changed. If there is a case where I need to spot deworm someone in the pasture who hasn't responded to this dewormer, I will switch to another one in that case. This is the only time I have ever changed dewormers. It used to be recommended that you rotate dewormers each time you deworm. Now it is widely accepted that you are better off using one sparingly until the parasites in your herd show resistance to it and then switch. This is what we have always done.

I have taken the FAMACHA training that instructs you how to eye score goats and deworm based on the amount of anemia present by the color of their eyelids. It is a very useful tool but honestly I don't eye score every goat. I use it to determine if a particular goat is wormy or having another problem. I might randomly check some goat's eyelid as we are deworming them. But usually, by only deworming twice a year, most of our does need dewormed each time. To grab the head and pull the eyelid back on several hundred goats is too physically demanding for one or two people. I am not saying that it isn't a good practice and I have heard of people doing several hundred a day. If you ask me if you should do this, I will say yes. But for me, in our operation, with limited time and manpower, it simply isn't always done.

If a goat can produce offspring and keep them alive until weaning I am satisfied with her at this point of our breeding system. If her eyelids are pale and she seems wormier than the others, I am not that concerned, unless she can no longer produce. I do have a microscope and I will occasionally take fecal samples. It is more of a way for me to tell if a goat that has diarrhea is wormy or if it has coccidiosis. These are the only two reasons that I have found for a goat to have diarrhea, unless they have been turned out on new lush pasture or have overeaten on grain. You can learn to check a fecal sample for worms using the "Meat Goat Production Handbook" from Langston University, http://www.luresext.edu/index.htm ,and get a decent microscope for about $200.

CHAPTER 3

JUST KIDDING

Every morning during kidding season is like the first day of school when you were a kid. It can be your best day or it could be your worst, depending on how things turn out. Beginning the morning by going out and seeing new born kids up and nursing their mothers is always exciting and makes the work of goats much easier. This is how it should be but not always how it is, or has been.

For a few years I dreaded walking out the door and checking the pastures, finding dead or abandoned kids and trying to find who might have just kidded so I could take them back home, put them in a small pen and pair them up. There are years I did a lot of nighttime checking, to keep track of who had a baby, tagging them so I could pair them back up if there was a problem. I would often carry colostrum with me to tube newborns and leave them with their mothers if my pens were full at home.

Thankfully that was several years ago and now, every year our kidding season gets easier and more trouble free. I believe this can only be due to the fact that I have been keeping my own doelings as replacement does and not buying any outside does, since most of those would be backyard does. This has cost us a great deal because we have been selling only a little more than half a kid crop, that being the buck kids, and the slower growing doelings. At one time I figured that all the money we made on the meat kids went to pay the expenses for all the does; any profit we made was reinvested in keeping our replacements.

> *You should realize that your own doelings are worth more to you as replacements — if you want to grow your herd — than they are to anyone else.*

We were keeping doelings to replace non-producing does that were leaving our herd in dramatic numbers. You should realize that your own doelings are worth more to you as replacements — if you want to grow your herd — than they are to anyone else. Maybe you could buy cheaper doelings at any goat sale and sell yours private treaty for more money, but those cheaper doelings will cost you much more than what you sold your own for, in production losses. Your worst doe that you have raised will often be better than anyone's best doe that you put in your management system. By keeping my own, they have already survived my management, or mismanagement, style. This cannot be stressed enough and it will prove evident in your kidding season.

I will begin putting my bucks out with the does during the last week of October. This will start my kidding season in the last half of March.

I used to put my bucks all out in one or two days but after a few years I realized that if I put my bucks out over a two or three week time period, then I wouldn't have all my kids hitting the ground at the same time. This not only spreads my work load out but it also means that all my goats are not in the heart of kidding season if bad weather comes for a few days.

March and April can still bring late snowstorms. Even 40-degree days and drizzling rain or thunderstorms can be very life threatening to baby goats hitting the ground. A five- or six-pound goat doesn't have enough body mass to stay warm for very long and must be licked off and up and nursing very quickly. If it is cold and wet you must have very good does that do their job and kids that have been bred for vigor and a will to live. By spreading the kidding season over several weeks in different pasture locations that I have, I will hopefully have good weather for many of them to be born, and when bad weather comes, I have fewer pastures kidding that are affected by it.

I put bucks in the pastures that are closest to my home first and then the ones farther away, those being 6-7 miles, where I may not be able to check as often, so hopefully the weather is better later in the month of April. Some pastures may have an old barn or shelters of some type and I will put the bucks out there earlier since they will have a little protection if the does kid earlier in April. Although, don't count on all those does going to the barn to kid.

How many does can one buck breed?

I usually start with putting only one buck in a herd that I want the most kids born from. I will call him my "first choice buck". These herds will range from 50-100 does on 40-160 acre pastures. I will leave him there and bring in another buck, a "backup" buck, after about 17-21 days. I figure the first buck will cover 40-50 does. I've had them cover more than that but you don't want to count on it every time. I figure one buck for 40-50 does but I always bring in a second one and I may even bring in a yearling buck that I have kept back out of my own herd the previous year after that. I always want the does exposed to at least two mature bucks as you never know if a buck is fertile or doing his job. I rarely see a buck actually breeding, occasionally you will catch one in the act, but don't worry, by using this method, I have never failed to have does kidding in the spring.

> *I always want the does exposed to at least two mature bucks as you never know if a buck is fertile or doing his job.*

How often do you kid?

I only kid once a year. Goats are seasonal breeders, meaning they can begin cycling when the days start getting shorter, June 21st. You will see many does cycling in August and September. If you leave your buck kids as intact males you will want to be weaning them by August. They will begin breeding your does and you will have kids born in Dec., Jan. and Feb. Not a good time for kids to hit the ground unless you are specifically prepared for it with heated barns and extra man-hours you can spend. That's another mistake I learned from experience, so you might as well learn from my mistake.

When beginning to look into the goat business and figuring a cash flow statement, I knew that gestation for a goat was 5 months and given that cattle can cycle again 60 days or sooner after giving birth, I thought we could get two or almost two kid crops a year. I was even told this by someone who was trying to sell me goats. Due to their seasonal breeding this is not normally true. I have personally known only one person who was successful in breeding goats out of season in order to get more than one kid crop a year here in the Midwest. He tried it for several years and was only recently successful on a small scale. True, I don't know everybody who has goats and I am sure some who are reading this have done this or know others who have been successful at it. If you do breed more than once a year, you must be ready to have some of these kids born in months when snow may be on the ground and cold weather is a daily occurrence. Your labor and frustration level will increase dramatically and so will your feed cost.

> *For larger Midwestern goat operations it is probably going to be more profitable to kid only once a year in the spring.*

For larger Midwestern goat operations it is probably going to be more profitable to kid only once a year in the spring. Spring grass is beginning to grow and support the nutritional needs of does that are beginning to produce milk and kids that will start picking at forage a few weeks after birth. If you kid later than April, say May or June, then you are going to be working with the last part of the breeding season as the days begin to get longer on Dec. 21ˢᵗ and more goats will cease to cycle as the days get longer. Your best conception rates will probably be to breed in October, November and December. I usually leave my bucks in until February or March when I am gathering my does and vaccinating and deworming them before kidding season. I very seldom get does that give birth later than the middle of May and 95% will be born before the end of April.

> *My does all kid in the pastures that they have been in all winter, spring, summer and fall.*

My does all kid in the pastures that they have been in all winter, spring, summer and fall. It seems to work best if you can have a group of does and guardian dogs that stay in the same pasture all the time. They learn where they're supposed to be and are more content there. That being said, you will need some small pens in a barn somewhere for kidding problems and for adoptions. I have six 5' x 5' pens in my barn at home.

Does and their kids in some small pens. These might be adoptions or just stressed kids that needed to be brought in and helped to nurse or some other problem.

How do you make adoptions?

Many times if I have triplets and I have a doe that lost her kids I will graft one of the triplets onto the other doe. Or if you have any other poor milking doe, or any reason to graft a kid onto another doe, it can be done relatively easy. I will usually take the strongest triplet away from their mother for the adoption. You want a kid that is strong and wanting to nurse. I'll then tube colostrum down him or let him get it from his own mother if she has plenty for three kids, then put him in the pen with the new mother. Don't put the two families in pens next to each other, where they can see and bawl at each other.

Sometimes you will get lucky and they will just get up and start nursing on their own. Most times you will have to hold the new mom for the kid and maybe put the nipple in his mouth as he is hunting around for it. Always make sure the adoptee mom has good milk flow. That may be the reason she lost her own kids. You may have to hold her very forcefully or maybe just a little. Use as little force as it takes, and then ease up on her as she lets the kid nurse. You may have to hold her the first day 3 or 4 times for the kid to nurse, hopefully using less holding force every time. Then I get a long cattle prod-type sorting stick; from outside the pen I will use it to prod the mother when she moves away from the kid, not letting it nurse. The kid will learn that when you show up he can go nurse and the doe will hold still or she gets prodded. After a while you will only need to stand there without the prod.

If you miss a feeding time and the kid is standing there bawling, you know she's not letting him nurse yet. If he is lying down content, then he has been nursing while you were away. When you see the kid lying at one end of the pen and the doe lying at the other, that is a sign that the mother is pushing him away and he's not able to nurse on his own yet. When they are lying together, that is almost always a good sign that he has nursed and she is accepting him.

This whole process will usually take 3-4 days at the most. Young, first-time kidding does will accept a kid very quickly, some older does are more of a challenge. I very seldom have an adoption failure. Adopting two new kids on a doe that has none is a similar process. It is more difficult to adopt a kid onto a mother that already has one of her own. It can be done but I seldom do, unless it is a young doe with a lot of milk and I have the time.

After she has accepted her new kid and they are doing well for a day or two in the small pen, I will turn them into a larger area, maybe a 50' x 50' pen. I seldom take them right back out to pasture. After I am confident about the new family, she will go back to pasture with her new kid.

If you have goats, you should learn how to tube baby goats. But I guess it's not something you can really practice, you will just learn as you go. You should get a kid tube and syringe. I like the tube that is soft rubber and the 120 cc syringe. You can get this at www.premier1supplies.com, or www.valleyvet.com, or other vet supply stores that carry goat supplies. You need to lay the kid down on his chest and stretch his neck out. I usually kneel down with them between my knees on the ground. Then stick the tube down his throat. If he bawls as it is going down, that is a good sign and you are in the right place. If he doesn't make any noise, you may be in the right place but you may not be. I say, pull it out and do it again, listening for his bawling as it is going down. You can also blow into the tube after it is inserted and see if his belly enlarges. If it doesn't then you are in the lungs and need to reinsert the tube. The tube should go down into the kid until only a couple inches are sticking out of his mouth.

If you get it in the lungs and force colostrum into them he will die within a few minutes. That used to happen to me about once a year. I would simply get in too big of a hurry. If it happens to you, you will feel sick about it as you were trying to help the kid and accidentally drowned him. You will need to get over it and not let it stop you from doing it the next time a kid is in distress. He will need your courage to keep him alive. Just be more careful.

Anytime I have to bring a newborn in because he's weak or stressed in some way, I milk the mom and tube the colostrum down the kid. He may nurse on his own, but this way I know he's got it and I can go to bed and not worry about him. I like to give a

> ### DO NOT MICROWAVE THE COLOSTRUM! IT WILL TURN THE ANTIBODIES INTO A GEL!

newborn 2 to 2.5 oz. of colostrum. That is why I like the bigger syringe so I can tube two kids with one syringe. Early in the kidding season you will want to milk any doe that has extra colostrum and keep it frozen.

To thaw out colostrum, I put some water in a bowl and microwave it to get it hot then put a plastic cup of frozen colostrum in the hot water. Do not Microwave The Colostrum! It will Turn the Antibodies into a Gel! Like me, you'll have to find out for yourself. I put the colostrum in plastic Solo cups of one dose and some cups of two doses so if I have a single or twins or triplets, I can thaw out just enough for what I need. I've also been told you can freeze it in ice cube trays and then put the cubes in a plastic bag and take out as many colostrum cubes as you need.

As you check new mothers out in pasture, you want to watch for kids that are humped up and appear to be standing on their tiptoes. These are kids that are hungry and who you will find dead in a day or two if you don't start supplementing them with a bottle or adopt them on another mother. His mother may have a bad bag or developed mastitis and it hurts her when the kid begins to nurse, so she kicks him off, or he may simply be a smaller kid and not getting his share because his big brother hogs all the milk. Whatever the reason, when you see this kid, he is much worse than he appears. Trust me. He may walk off or even run but he's just trying to fool you into leaving him alone.

If you find a kid that is too weak to stand up, there is one thing I've found that will often get him going again. If he is too weak to stand then my experience is that tubing milk down him won't help him. It is as though his body has shut down and he won't digest milk any longer. You will want to have "Lactated Ringers" on hand. This can only be obtained with a veterinarian prescription and consists of electrolytes in an I.V. bag solution. You will also need 50% dextrose solution. This can be bought over the counter at some farm supply stores or a veterinarian. I take a 60-cc syringe and draw 10-15 cc's of dextrose into it, and then draw the syringe full with the Lactated Ringers. You need to inject all of this under the skin of his neck or shoulder. They don't like this and will bawl loudly but it is for their own good.

Make sure to feel his mouth. If his mouth feels cold then you need to warm him. I don't like heat lamps as well as a heater that actually blows hot air on the kid. I often put them in the cab of the pickup with me as I am driving around checking other pastures. I also have a wooden box made for them and a place for a small electric bathroom type heater to sit behind a partition so the kid won't tip it over. It is even better if you take the time to immerse them in warm water then thoroughly blow dry him. You will want to "ringer" him again every couple hours and let him suck or tube him when he is able to stand. I have actually brought kids back from the brink of death this way. Make sure to get them a new mother the first chance you get, bottle feeding them until then. Don't put them back on their own mom, as you won't get a chance to revive them more than once.

> *you won't get a chance to revive them more than once.*

Do you have to assist many does during kidding?

Occasionally you will have a doe that is having a problem kidding. The kid is not coming out properly and the doe has been in labor for longer than normal. If I see a doe that is off by herself but not straining, I will check her again in a couple hours. I won't get too concerned until I see her in actual labor and trying to push. At this point I will give her maybe an hour, depending on how busy I am.

The next time I see her I want to see some type of progress. I should at least see a foot or even just the water sack starting to come out. In reality, she should have had the kid by now, but some take longer than others, so as long as she is making progress of some kind, I'm OK with that. After another hour, if she hasn't had the kid, I will catch her and reach inside to help.

You may only get a few fingers inside the birth canal or maybe your hand up to the knuckles. This makes it very challenging but keep working at it. You might want to lubricate your hands with dish soap to try to reach in farther or to slide the kid out. You may find that there is a front leg turned back, which is the most common. You simply need to pull the leg forward. You may have to push the kid back in to do that. If the head is turned back you will have to push the kid back and then turn the head forward. I have seen does that will have an ear sticking out of the birth canal, meaning the head of the kid is turned sideways, or a tail sticking out, meaning the kid is coming backwards and the back feet are pointing forward or towards the mothers head. These you should help immediately. I have had some does give birth to a kid coming backwards by themselves, but only if the back feet are coming out first. It is a lot of stress on both of them and the kid may not get up and suck for some time.

There are a few occasions when you simply cannot help the doe. The kid is coming with a head back or some other presentation that won't allow her to give birth and you cannot get your hand in far enough to move him so he can come out. I will put these in a pen and try to help them every few hours.

You may have to determine yourself if you want to take the doe to the veterinarian for a c-section. It will probably cost more than the doe is worth and the kid will usually be dead by this time.

I usually have only 2 or 3 I have to help in the course of a year. Rarely will I have one that I cannot help out. By continuing to try and help her during the course of the day, you will give her time to dilate more fully and rest between sessions.

I had a doe that I put in the kidding pen in this exact situation. I had tried to help her several times during the day. A friend of mine asked me if he could butcher her and I agreed. He was to be out early the next day. That morning I went to check her and she had triplets up and nursing. Sometimes things work out.

More than once I've had a doe that I had caught to assist, three-leg tying them and loading them in the back of the pickup to take back home. They gave birth before I made it out the gate. I recently read an article that said old timers used to let the doe out of the pen and have their herding dog run her around, jostling the kid inside the doe and that on many occasions the doe would kid by herself.

If you assist any doe giving birth, you should always milk her out and tube the kid with colostrum. I have found that some does that need assistance, especially first-time kidders, will have very thick colostrum that will be hard for the kid to suck. In that case you'll need to thaw your frozen colostrum and give these a couple ounces. Making sure the kid has had colostrum will eliminate one of your worries for the day. You may ask your veterinarian for some oxytocin to help these does come to their milk.

When do you castrate buck kids?

When I had fewer goats I would castrate at birth. I know many people will say that this is not a good practice and that you will have more urinary calculi problems later on, but I simply did not want to handle the kids again before weaning, and at weaning it is a very hot time of the year and the stress on these kids is severe enough that I don't want to castrate then. I don't believe I ever lost a kid to urinary calculi (kidney stones), at least that I know of. But maybe I was just lucky. Now I do not castrate at all. The selling price for a buck kid is usually the same as a wether. Castrating bucks is simply one more thing to do that doesn't seem as important as other things do at that time. That being said, if I had fewer goats I would again castrate at birth when I am tagging the kid, either cutting with a knife or banding with a calf castration band. That would keep the buck kids from riding the doelings and even each other while you're feeding post weaning. Of course, it's hard to keep any bucks for your own breeding stock if you do this.

Do you ear tag all those kids?

I try to tag the kids with their mother's number. If I don't catch them the first day after birth they are usually too fast for me, so many go without tags. I may never know how many kids I have from a group of does until I wean them. I have recently come

I have recently come to find out that tagging a kid for my own records isn't the most important thing. Having a live kid to sell is.

to find out that tagging a kid for my own records isn't the most important thing. Having a live kid to sell is. This thought has changed my ideas about tagging and identifying the kids.

I won't tag kids during a stressful weather situation, cold, wet or rainy. During bad weather having them paired up with their mother is more important than getting a tag on them. When you stop to tag the kid in an open pasture you run the risk of one kid running one way and the other one going another, wandering aimlessly across an open pasture with a tag on. I have spent too much time trying to pair up a family after I upset them by tagging the kids. I also don't like to tag one close to dark as they will bawl very loudly and call every predator in the county, just making the livestock guardian dog's job much harder. I swear I have had one of the dogs standing by me while I was tagging a kid late in the evening that began to bawl, sounding like a world class predator call. The dog looked at me and said, "Now you went and did it, it's going to be a long night".

If I do attempt to tag a doe's kids, I will approach her very quietly from the side, not walking straight at her. I will crouch down, attempting to make myself smaller and less threatening to her. Down on my knees I will hold the kids, tagging males in the right ear and females in the left very quickly with the tags that I already have made out. After tagging one, hold it tightly as you tag the other one. Do not release one kid until you are done tagging all of them. The mother may walk off with only that one. You should tag both kids and lay them back down together, hoping that they will stay down and the mother will come up to them before they get up and split, running off randomly. If they do, try to do your best to pair them back up as a family. This isn't easy and sometimes the more you try the worse things become.

Another rule I have learned to follow is that I will never disturb a kid or pair when I find them alone in the pasture without a

> *Do not release one kid until you are done tagging all of them.*

doe around. I have grown in confidence in my does and if the kids look licked off then I trust that the doe knows where they are. If they have just been born and abandoned, not licked off, I will look the does over to try and decide who the mom might be. If I can determine that, then I will catch her and take them both back to a small pen. You can take a bucket of feed and bring the whole herd back to where the kid is but not feed them. Get the kid up and make him bawl then see if someone comes to claim him. A kid that is not licked off may not have his mother come back to him later. Make sure that you don't bring the wrong doe, one that has a kid hid out somewhere else. If you do you may end up with two problems instead of one. If I'm unsure of his mother, I will take him home and get colostrum down him, bottle-feeding him until I can graft him onto another mother. You can continue to check the pasture for his mother, as she may be bawling for a kid or some other clue that she is truly his mother. This will take some experience and savvy on your part. Even then, you'll make the wrong call on occasion, trust me on this one.

Ironically, I have noticed that I have better kidding percentages in the does that I let kid in the pasture than the ones I keep in smaller paddocks to try and check more often. That could be because they are first-time kidders that I move home and the pastures there get used more heavily and have a higher level of parasite population. But this is just an observation with no recommendation at this time.

There are some tricks that I use when I am trying to catch a goat in a herd so I can assist it in birth, doctor it, or have any reason to handle her or three-leg tie her like a calf and take her back home for any reason.

It is made easier if you carry some feed in a bucket with you and can get the doe to come to the feed with several other does crowding around her. If she is off by herself sick or having a kidding problem, then bring the whole herd to her and put some feed on the ground near her. Wait and let the other does come

> *Simply act like you don't want her, then quickly reach forward and grab her back leg as her head is down eating.*

and eat. Be patient and wait for her to put her head down. Don't stare at her or look her in the eye. Goats know they are prey and sense when they are about to be preyed upon. Look away from her while keeping track of her out of the corner of your eye as you are walking around behind her. Simply act like you don't want her, then quickly reach forward and grab her back leg as her head is down eating. You want your first shot at catching her to succeed because she won't be as easy to catch once she knows you're after her. Like most animals, goats seem to have a sense something is up, once you are trying to catch them. I also keep a goat "hook" in my pickup, a 4-foot aluminum rod with a crook on the end, that I can often snag their back leg with. You can purchase these wherever you get goat supplies. One that extends to 6 or 7 foot is nice and you can get pretty good using it with a little practice. If your good with a rope that works too.

I also carry one of my Border Collies with me all the time. Many times just by getting him out of the pickup the doe will watch him and I can get my hands on her. If not, he will catch that doe and hold her by the front, or back leg until I can get to her.

Sometimes I feel like my whole business relies on my dogs. Guard dogs and herding dogs are an important asset in my business. You could get by without them but I wouldn't want to.

CHAPTER 4

WHAT TYPE OF WORKING FACILITIES DO I NEED?

When we first started in goats and had a couple hundred head of does, deworming and vaccinating was done by hiring some of my son's friends. After crowding the goats in a small barn, we would grab them and hold the goat as medications were administered and a mark put on the goats head to signify that it had been treated. After a few years of that, I got some gates from a hog farm that was going out of business and set them up in a temporary fashion to make an alleyway and a small pen from which we pushed them into the ally. All this was temporary. I have a saying: "Everything is temporary unless it works." I am sure we have run tens of thousands of goats through that temporary alleyway since that day. We have modified it some but it is basically the same.

> *"Everything is temporary unless it works."*

Weaned goats waiting to be dewormed, vaccinated and weighed in our "temporary" goat-working alleyway.

The alleyway is 40 feet long and about 36" high. You don't want it so high that it is hard to reach over to administer shots.

You don't want it so low that the goats constantly jump over it. We will occasionally get one that jumps out, maybe one for every 150 – 200 that go through it. It is about 16 inches – 20 inches wide, as it's been spread over the years in a few areas. Does can turn around in it but it is difficult for them. If you make it too narrow, the goats won't want to move down it very well. It needs to be wide enough for the pregnant does to go through for revaccination in February and March before they kid in April. Ours is pointed slightly downhill as that helps them flow through it better. In the end that they load from, there is a plywood door that has one side wired onto the alley like a hinge that pushes forward as they push on it but when they try to back up, it wedges between the two walls of the alleyway.

> *If you make it too narrow, the goats won't want to move down it very well.*

When we work the does or kids, we crowd them into the alley and deworm and give vaccinations by walking up and down the alley with an automatic syringe gun loaded with vaccine, shooting them in the neck and shoulder area. We don't use any kind of goat chute or head catch. It seems to me that catching every goat would be too slow. I can usually run through 75 kids in an hour and weigh them also. We normally put about 20, or so, does in the alley at one time, almost twice that many weaned kids.

To weigh them I set scales at the end of the alley and have another gate behind the scales with a rope that will raise the gate up as I push a goat onto the scales. It's good information to know what your goats weigh before you sell them so there are not many surprises.

The scales sit in the alley and the gate is set in behind the scales. You can also see part of another gate behind the scales that we put in so we could keep four or five goats up closer to the scales and not have to walk all the way back to the end of the alley for the last 10 or 15 head.

At the end of this alleyway there is a three-way sorting gate that I made. It has a gate that raises with a rope. They can go straight out to one pen, and there is a door on each side that will turn them to the right into another pen or to the left into another pen. I can pull these gates open with ropes while pushing them through the gate if I am working by myself. This is the easiest way we have found to sort kids from the does or sort buck kids from doe kids. Goats are small and quick and the only other way to effectively sort them is often by physically catching them in a small pen and dragging them out the gate.

The 3-way sorting gate at the end of the alley. The front gate raises and the gates on each side push in to steer the goats out to one side or the other.

The pens we have at home to hold goats for various reasons are made from wire cattle panels with 6-inch x 6-inch squares. Goats will often get their heads caught in these panels but the 4 inch x 4 inch square panels are very expensive. I do have some of those where we wean the kids. You can simply use steel "T" posts placed 8 feet apart to hold these up. You may want the post closer if you are using them in a crowding pen.

I like to have a catch pen in every goat pasture. You are more likely to catch the goats when you need to if you already have a pen there and don't have to move your panels from another location. It is usually blistering hot the time we need to wean the kids in late July and August. If I have to move and set up a goat pen it often makes me want to procrastinate on the whole process. It takes about 10 – 12 panels to make a catch pen and trailer-loading alley in the pasture for 100 or so goats and their kids. We usually bring the goats home to work or wean them and there are often some that need sorted off. Our facilities at home are much easier on the goats and goat handlers.

Do you trim hooves in the alley?

I have my does sign a contract with me when they enter the herd as a breeding doe. It simply states that as long as they can efficiently eat, drink and raise a kid, I will leave their feet alone.

I know that some people routinely catch all their does and trim their hooves and I have read countless articles about how often and how important it is to trim your doe's hooves. I believe this is a good idea for some. For me, it is a chore that I never want to get started. I will trim hooves on any doe that I have to individually catch for any other reason, spot deworming, helping one in the kidding process or any other problem. If I have her caught I will probably trim her hooves if needed. Since you have her caught anyway you might as well make the best of it.

I have read that goats shouldn't be allowed to stand in mud or poorly drained areas. This may be a viable option for back-yard goats but for pasture goats that must drink from a pond or creek, it simply doesn't make sense. I believe foot rot is a genetic problem as much as an environmental one. I have had times of wet weather where it seemed like there were more does limping than walking normally, but then even in dry weather you can have problems. I have bad feet on rocky pastures as well as those that have no rocks. I have small kids get foot rot as well as aged does. Many will get over it on their own. If they don't then I treat them. Some get sold later and others I'll never recognize as a previous limper.

If I have a doe in a pasture that seems to be continually limping and it is interfering with her ability to forage, I will usually catch her and trim her hooves. At this point her hoof would be infected. This is commonly called foot rot or hoof scald, depending on who is talking about it. Prying her hooves apart you will likely see a red irritation that smells bad. The affected hoof will be severely grown out by this time. It will be very hard and difficult to cut. You will want to have the heavy white handled hoof trimmers for this job. The smaller orange handled hoof trimmers are very good if you trim hooves on a regular basis, before they get really out of control.

When the hoof is infected I'll usually put iodine and Koppertox on the hoof or a 50/50 mixture of Clorox and water and give her an antibiotic injection. I normally carry these items with me in the pickup so I have it as I am checking my does. If it is a dry doe or in the fall of the year I will catch her and put her on feed to fill her out then send her to the sale when I have 20 head or so. If she has a kid, I'll let her raise it but I will take my knife and cut the tip of her ear off. This is a mark I put on any doe that I am considering culling for any reason but may want to give her another chance. If a doe with a cut off ear limps again or gives me any other reason to question her reliability as a producing doe, I sell her. I don't know if anyone else uses this marking system but if you are ever at a sale and see a group of does go through the ring with tipped off ears, buyer beware. On second thought, buyer beware of any doe brought to the sale barn. Someone once told me, "there may be some good ones there but all the bad ones are there."

> *"there may be some good ones there but all the bad ones are there."*

If you looked at the hooves of the goats on my place, many you would think need trimming, but some would look like they are trimmed regularly. It doesn't necessarily correspond to their productivity. If you want to trim the hooves of your goats, I would recommend that you do so, and you may have less foot problems, but you may have goats with bad feet that need regular trimming to be productive.

CHAPTER 5

PREDATOR CONTROL

"We used to have llamas" or "We used to have burros or don-keys", was the response I got when I would ask goat producers how they protected their investment in goats from predators.

When we started into meat goat production, I wanted to use anything but Livestock Guardian Dogs, for protecting the herds. Burros or llamas would be simpler. They'd eat the same thing the goats would, and keeping them in the pasture would not be an issue due to the fencing required for goats. Although against my earlier plans, I was soon convinced that it would have to be dogs protecting our goats in a pasture situation.

I do not have firsthand experience with burros or llamas but I am told that they do not necessarily bond to the goats although they have a natural dislike for coyotes or dogs and will run them off. In my opinion, for larger pasture situations, this would not be an adequate way to protect goats. The goats may be more than a mile away from the protection at times, or a doe, off by herself kidding or tending to her kid. Not to take anything away from someone who is using another type of predator control, but for us, it seemed that Livestock Guardian Dogs (LGDs) were the best choice for the most reliable protection on the pastures we were putting goats out on.

I have had neighbors ask me how I train those dogs to round up the goats every night as soon as the coyotes start howling. The guardian dogs are very amazing animals. They may lie around all day and you wonder if they even are worth the food they eat. But come nightfall they will often herd the goats to a hilltop or open area where they can see and ward off any intruders.

When I check my goats and I don't see one of the dogs, I keep looking because they will usually be lying beside a goat who is off by itself for some reason, often times having a problem I can help with. I would probably not have known the doe was there if it wasn't for wondering where the dog was.

Do you have to train the dogs?
Livestock Guardian Dogs are bred to want to stay with what they are raised among, just like a hunting dog is bred to hunt. It's simply part of their breed characteristics. If I have goats get out for some reason, the dog will be right there with them. Training them could actually be detrimental to the bonding relationship with the goats. Simply put them with goats in a small pen when they are weaned or even before if that's possible and let them do what they are bred to do.

You should try to get a dog and the goats at the same time; buying them from the same herd is best but not often possible. If that can't be done, then you should get the goats first and the dog as soon as possible. If you get a pup and don't have any goats, he will bond with whatever he is around. That may be you or your children, or even a family pet. If you get an older LGD that has been with goats but you haven't gotten any yet, he will be very nervous and anxious. He may run off to look for goats to be with. LGDs are another part of the business that you must learn to deal with

> *LGDs are another part of the business that you must learn to deal with if you are to be successful with pasture goats.*

if you are to be successful with pasture goats. You must be able to handle these large dogs but not make them pets.

I believe these dogs truly know they are there to guard and protect the goats. They stay in the pastures all year long, lying among the goats and staying warm with the kids in brush or behind natural windbreaks in the winter. Each dog has its own personality that you need to know and deal with. We have over 20 dogs looking over our herds. We wouldn't need as many if all our goats were in one herd in one pasture but they run in 8-10 pastures of 40 – 160 acres with 50 – 100 breeding does in each pasture. We mostly have two and sometimes three dogs in each pasture, at least during kidding season. During kidding and when the kids are very young, they are the most vulnerable to predators. A predator can come in and snatch a kid that is off sleeping by itself on the other side of the pasture, before a dog may know it is near. I've often found a dog lying with a kid that has gotten separated from the herd. It seems that during kidding time we never have enough dogs but the rest of the year we have too many. Each dog will eat about 15 bags of dog food a year. You do the math, how many kids do they have to save you to make back what they cost?

I like a dog that is not overly friendly but who will let me catch him to deworm him or put him in the cab of the pickup to move him if I need him somewhere else. You need to socialize a young pup to get him this way but not make a pet out of him. It is OK to pet him in the pasture but never let him come to the house or other area where you don't want them to stay. Don't pet or feed him there or do anything but chase him vigorously back to where he belongs immediately.

I used to let the mother raise the pups in the goat pasture until they were several months old. She would teach them the trade. This was fine but as I got busier with more goats I wasn't able to take the time to socialize them and I had some grown dogs that wouldn't let me catch them. They weren't mean, just elusive. Now, I would rather bring the pups home to wean them and put them in a pen where I keep a few goats that have been sick or one problem or another. I can then socialize them and they learn how to eat out of the self-feeding dog food feeder. I will take them out to pasture after a few months.

You may notice that the pup, as it is going through the "adolescence" stage of its growth, may chase kids around playfully and even chew on their ears or be rough on them in some other way. Most all pups will go through this stage. I try not to have any young dogs where I have newborn kids but this isn't always possible. Some people think the older dogs will keep the pups from playfully hurting the kids. That would be nice but it doesn't always hold true.

If I have a pup that is playfully rough housing my kids, I will take a 2 x 4 about 2 feet long and attach it to about one foot of chain with an eyehook in the middle of the board. I then clip this to his collar. As he runs and chases the kids he will bang this between his legs. Don't let it dangle on the ground on too long of a chain or it may get caught in trees or brush. You will have to feed the dog by hand because it won't be jumping into the dog food feeder with the board on. If I have to have a pup with new kids, I try to have him here at home so I can watch him and feed him if I have to use the board treatment. It may take a few weeks or a month until he gets over this or the kids are big enough he no longer bothers them.

Ask your veterinarian to recommend a dewormer for your LGDs and how to prevent heartworms. Of course you will want to keep their rabies vaccinations current.

Occasionally I will have a dog get a "hot spot" on them. It is a sore that they get and continue to irritate from scratching or rubbing. They will sometimes get them even in the winter. You can put any topical antibiotic cream on it and fly spray if it is fly season. For extremely bad cases my vet recommended a penicillin injection for three days. It is more prevalent in long hair dogs but can affect even some short hair breeds.

What's your favorite breed of LGD?

I really like my Akbash dogs, their hair is short and they seem to have a good disposition, socializing very easily and take being handled or moved from herd to herd quite well. We do have some Anatolian Shepherds and crosses of the two and they are great dogs, also. I have some Komondor dogs. They look like huge poodles. I love their disposition and the way they stay with the goats but their hair is very long and gets matted and they are more prone to get hot spots or have fleas. But I certainly wouldn't let that stop me from getting another one if I had the chance.

I'm not terribly fond of Great Pyrenees; they are perimeter guardians and some will roam outside of the pasture, causing problems if you have smaller pastures with close neighbors. We had one that was actually killing our goats and another half Pyrenees that chewed the tails off of some. That being said, we have one Great Pyrenees, she's black, and she is probably our best dog. So maybe it is hit or miss with any breed.

At some of my pasture locations I have neighbors that have dogs and there seems to be an adjustment period between the neighbor's housedogs and my guardian dogs. After a few weeks they usually work things out. The neighbor's dog may come up to my fence and the dogs bark at each other, but it's usually not a problem. Sometimes, when I would have a dog that would go roam to the neighbor's house, I would take that dog to another pasture and bring in another one. Sometimes you will get personality clashes that just can't be worked out any other way. Once I get a set of dogs that are settled into a herd of goats and they know their surroundings and where they should be, I really don't like to move them anywhere else unless it is unavoidable.

> *Once I get a set of dogs that are settled into a herd of goats and they know their surroundings and where they should be, I really don't like to move them anywhere else unless it is unavoidable.*

Will a Livestock Guardian Dog attack people?

Occasionally I will have someone ask me if "those dogs" will attack people. My answer varies. If it is someone who I don't want in my pasture I will tell them, "Yes they will. You definitely should stay away from them." If it is someone who wants to take their kids in and look at my kids, I will tell them, "No, probably not, they may bark at you and not like you around the goats, but I've not had one that I thought would attack a person, but, they are an animal and they can be unpredictable so always use caution." I usually know my dogs and the temperament of each one. Some will come up and want attention from a stranger like a pet, others will bark and just simply stay back away from the person intruding his pasture. If someone wants to come and look at the kids during kidding season, I usually have them come to my home place. I will certainly have some in the pens in the barn, making adoptions or taking care of some problem.

If someone is going in the pasture to fish or cut firewood, the goats and dogs will mostly just stay away. I've had people tell me they have stopped along the road to look at the goats across the fence and the dogs came and barked at them. This is what I would want them to do.

> *I would be apprehensive about someone going into the pasture at night.*

I would be apprehensive about someone going into the pasture at night. These dogs get much more aggressive after the daylight hours when they can't see what the intrusion is and predators are on the prowl. They have made me a believer in their effectiveness when I have been checking the goats after dark. They will be ferociously defending the herd even from me, until they recognize my voice.

Is it best to have a male or female LGD?

I don't think the sex of the dog really matters. I have males that are very good and females that are just as good. For me it would be easier if all the dogs were neutered or spayed. If I could buy all the LGDs that I need, when I need them, I don't think I would ever keep breeding stock. But sometimes this isn't possible. I usually keep one or two breeding pairs. Raising and selling pups is just one more thing I don't have time for but I sometimes find it necessary to replace my own dogs. Just like you and me, they will grow old quicker than you think. I have a couple dogs that are 10 years old. I don't like to use them by themselves, but they are great to pair with a younger dog. With smaller pastures here in the Midwest, the dogs don't have to travel too far while doing their job, and just their presence will mostly deter coyotes, who are our main problems.

How do you feed so many dogs?

To feed our dogs we use a self-feeder that holds 50 lbs. of dog food and put cattle panels around it making a small pen maybe a 7-ft. x 7-ft. square. You must make it large enough so the dog doesn't feel trapped when he goes in to eat. Then cut a hole in the panels about two feet off the ground. It is best if you have a board wired to the panel from the ground to the bottom of the hole so the dog won't get his feet caught in the panel. Although I've never had this happen it is a fear of mine to find a dog that has been hanging in the dog food feeder for a few days. I like to put it close to the road so people driving by might see if that has happened and call me. Also, putting chicken wire around it will keep the goats from sticking their heads in the panel and getting caught. For some older dogs I will take a 2-ft. x 4-ft. piece of plywood and cut an oval hole in it a couple feet off the ground. I then attach a couple 2" x 2" cleats to it so the dog can help itself in and out of the feeder.

Occasionally a goat will figure out there is free food in there. I have some dogs that will not let goats near the feeder and others that don't seem to mind if one jumps in and eats.

I have taken a piece of plastic pipe a couple feet long and duct taped it across the horns of a goat so she couldn't jump through the hole.

Buck, an Anatolian Shepherd X Akbash, eating
from the self-feeder after jumping through the hole.

If you are like me and get tired of buying expensive dog collars only to have your dogs lose them, you might try this. Get some small chain and a snap or clasp of some sort. Cut it to fit the dog and leave a couple inches dangling to adjust it as he grows. I also attach a cattle ear tag to the collar with my name and phone number on it written with a tag ink marker. If your dog gets lost and can't remember your phone number he can always look at the tag and call you to come get him.

I should mention here that I have two Border Collies that I use to round up my goats when I want to catch them. A good LGD will not like strange dogs in the goat pasture so I will spend some time getting the LGDs used to the Border Collies. They will learn that when these dogs are with me it is OK. They don't necessarily like it but they tolerate the herding dogs. I have had to break up a fight or two among the herding dogs and LGDs. It's hard to get mad at a guard dog for doing his job but my herding dogs are a great asset and I don't want to risk their health. You might want to chain the guard dog if you think you will have trouble. But if they are not used to being on a chain you might create another problem.

CHAPTER 6

KEEPING 'EM IN

People always ask me if you can make any money raising goats. I tell them that if you can keep 'em in and keep 'em alive then you are at least more likely to make money. So let's start with the easiest one first.

We use electric wire put up in front of a barbed wire type cow fence that was already keeping cows in, or supposed to.

The first goat fence we made, we put two strands of electric wire attached to the post between the barbed wire. We found out this isn't the best way to run the wire. The goats will sometimes stick their head through the electric wire, get shocked, and then lift up and snag the electric wire on the barbed wire and short out the fence line. We now put the electric wire 12 inches or so out in front of the barbed wire on fiberglass post. This keeps it from being so close to the barbed wire, getting caught on it and shorting out. This is by far our best method for fencing goats on pasture. It is the most cost effective and most effective at keeping them in that we have used.

One pasture that I had cattle on, the landlord asked me if he bought the wire and helped us fence it, if we would bring our goats over there to eat the brush and weeds. There was no 110-volt electricity available so we decided to put up extra strands of barbed wire on the existing fence. We added 3 wires and made an 8 barbed wire fence. We have since put electric wire around this pasture with a 12-volt charger. Even with eight barbed wires it was the only pasture where our goats would get out more than occasionally. It is rare that I get a goat out through the electric wire. This method works well if you have any resemblance of a cow fence behind the electric wire. If there is no fence we run three strands of wire with the middle one a ground. We have now gone to one strand of electric in front of a barbed wire fence as our goats are so used to it they don't want near it. There are a few things we've learned along the way in building electric fence that will make it easier for us to check and maintain.

> *If you have limited time to spend hunting down a short in your fence you will want to invest in a Fault Finder.*

If you have limited time to spend hunting down a short in your fence you will want to invest in a Fault Finder. They can be bought online at various fencing supply companies. I buy much of my supplies from www.kencove.com. This tool will help you to find a short or fault in your fence very quickly. There are ways we build our fence and direct our electricity that help us use the Fault Finder more effectively.

When we run our wires to a corner and begin to turn the corner to go another direction, we start with another corner insulator and begin our wire again instead of keeping it in one piece and running it around the corner and on to the next leg of fence. Keep the tail of our wire long enough to reach the next run of fence. Put some bends or coils in the wire to make it more like a spring and slide an insultube on it for a handle, and then put a hook in the wire. We use this as a jumper wire between the two runs of fence line hooking it across the corner. If there is a problem with the fence we can go to any corner and unhook the jumper and work on that leg of the fence without worrying about getting shocked. We can also disconnect the power to any pasture that we are not using at the time and direct our energy to another pasture.

Jumper wires connecting two runs of fence at a corner. You can see the insultube on the ends of the jumpers that are used for a handle.

On two-wire fences, we place a jumper wire between the top and bottom wire so you can disconnect the bottom wire if there becomes a grass load on it, keeping the top wire energized. This jumper will be an insulated wire or a wire with an insultube on it so we can easily remove it when needed. It also helps us to more effectively isolate a short in the fence. Knowing it is on the bottom or the top by disconnecting the bottom and taking a reading on the fence line with the Fault Finder. We make sure the path of the electricity is flowing in the same direction for the bottom and the top wire. This makes the Fault Finder much easier to use to find a problem.

Don't put the wire in a continuous loop. If you have a gate that you use to drive into the pasture it is nice to have both ends of your electric wire ending there. You can check the end of the fence and see how hot it is and check the beginning of the fence and let the Fault Finder tell you if you are losing voltage down the line. You can put the charger any place along the fence line, on the end or in the middle, but it is much easier to find a short if you have the electric wire stopping at the end of the fence and not running in a loop.

When learning to use the Fault Finder, think of your electric fence as pipe carrying water and a fault or short is where there is a leak in the pipe. The Fault Finder will tell you how much pressure is in the pipe at the point where you are testing it, and how much is leaking out of the pipe from the point you are at, to the end of the pipe. You simply move down the fence and test it again until you see the pressure drop or the voltage drops, and then you know you've passed the short, or leak in the pipe. We then come back to where we get the higher reading again and move down the line in the direction of electric flow until we get the low reading again. By isolating the fault between two points in the fence, then going back and forth taking readings with the Fault Finder, narrowing our search area, we can find a problem very quickly even on miles of fence line with multiple wires. Ultimately, we find the leak or short in the fence. With miles of fence on many different pasture sites, being proficient with this tool and knowing our fence, we can maintain it easily.

If we encounter a hinged swinging gate that we want to continue to use, and is goat proof or can be made goat proof by wiring cattle panels or 6 x 12 woven wire, then we will use insulated electric wire and put it in a PVC pipe and bury it under the gate. It doesn't have to be buried too deeply. We have even used insulated electric wire and put it inside a garden hose and laid it on top of the ground. It gets driven over but so far this is working well too. We just need a way to get the electricity to the other side of the gate and on down the fence line. This keeps us from having to disconnect a wire gate and open another gate to get into the pasture. I have seen people take the wire up and over the top of a gate and down the other side. I guess this would work also but I prefer going under the gate or on the ground. It really seems simpler.

An electric wire gap-type gate.

If your pasture has a wire gap-type gate, it can be replaced by an electric wire gap gate made from 2" PVC pipe with poly wire strung between it and 1" PVC pipe for gate stays. We use 3 or 4 strands of wire on these gaps and then connect each strand vertically with a steel wire wrapped from one then down to the next, so all wires are energized. We connect it to the run of fence on each side and there are various ways to do that using insulated electric wire that runs down the post. We put a hook in the insulated wire that hooks into the steel wire that is vertical and woven between the poly wires. This lets us unhook the electric wire so we can open the PVC gate.

An electric wire gap that is being energized by the
electric fence, using an insultube for a handle to
un-energize it and open the gate.

To make a water gap over a creek crossing we usually just run the main electric wire straight across the creek at whatever height it naturally wants to run, and then drop wires down through the creek using poly wire, tying it to the main electric wire on each side of the water gap. You may need to run two or three drop wires and put a few post in the creek bottom. Goats would have to be very hungry to walk through water that is even a few inches deep, so by just going to the normal water level is sufficient. If it is a two-wire fence we would drop wires off the bottom electric wire and could disconnect the whole bottom strand from electricity, by removing a jumper wire, when the water gets over it so it isn't shorting out the entire fence. Goats won't normally walk through water, so your gap is safe as long as the water is over it. You can easily go back

> **Goats won't normally walk through water, so your gap is safe as long as the water is over it.**

and fix the poly wire gap or just scrap it and start over when the water is down.

For most of my fences, I like to use 3/8 fiberglass posts and the clips that come with them. They don't work well in areas where there is a lot of upward or downward pressure on the wire, like when going over a hill. In those areas we will put steel "T" posts with pin-lock insulators. There also are larger fiberglass posts that can be used economically. I have even cut 6 ½-foot "T" posts in half and used them for electric fence posts. To tighten the wire we simply pull it as tight as we can by hand then use "Daisy" tighteners in the line. These are tightened with a ½ ratchet wrench.

How high do you put the electric wires?

It really isn't all that critical. Once the goats get used to the electric fence they won't be trying it, no matter if your wire is a little too high or too low. I would say that our top wire is 18 inches to 24 inches high and the bottom wire is at 12 inches or so. Don't make the bottom too low as you will get more grass load on the wire. For the single wire fence I would say it runs between 15" and 20" high, but I wouldn't recommend a single wire fence unless your goats are used to a hot wire.

Does the charger shock through weeds and grass?

Most chargers will shock through some grass as it grows up onto your fence, but with a few miles of fence and a spring time grass load you will notice the fence will not be as "hot" as it was before the grass started growing.

To keep a heavy weed load off our electric wires, we spray under our electric fence using 2 oz. Round Up, 2 oz. 2-4d and 2 oz. Pramitol per gallon of water. If there are woody plants that need to be sprayed, I would add 2 oz. of Remedy per gallon. Most fence lines can be sprayed from a 4-wheeler; hard to reach areas can be accessed using a backpack sprayer.

Why don't my goats stay inside my electric fence?

There are some common problems I have seen with an electric fence that won't keep goats in.

First I would want to know what kind of fence charger you have. You must have a powerful charger. I probably over power my fence, but that is always better than under powering it and having problems with livestock getting out.

> *Be prepared to spend more than you planned for a fence energizer.*

Be prepared to spend more than you planned on for a fence energizer. If we spend an extra $300 for a charger that is twice as powerful as what we maybe could get by with, that we'll have 10 years, that is $30/year; we may have 100 goats in that pasture so that is an extra 30 cents / goat / year. That's not much money to know that we will have a charger more than adequate to keep us from getting calls from people telling me that our goats are out. You may get by with a weaker charger as long as the fence doesn't have any grass load on it or any other problems, but that is rarely the case. On a 50-acre pasture I have a 6-joule charger, on an 80-acre pasture I have a 10-joule charger and on a 160-acre place I have a 20-joule charger. At our home place we have several pastures splitting over 400 acres but they are seldom energized all at the same time. We can disconnect any pasture we are not using. There is a 20-joule charger in my shop that powers the entire fence here at home. It also goes under a road in two places, and then to two pastures we rent across the road. Some people like fast cars, I like powerful chargers.

I like the Stafix chargers because with the remote control feature, the charger can be shut off using the hand held remote that also is a Fault Finder. By simply touching the fence anywhere along it and pressing the off button, I can turn the charger off. Working on the fence with the charger turned off is very, very handy. When you get shocked a few times hooking the wire back into an insulator, you will understand why the goats don't get out. We also have Taylor chargers that are very good and a little cheaper but no remote, so you just have to go to any corner and disconnect the jumper wire to work on a particular leg of fence.

Do not be fooled when the charger says that it will charge 50 miles or 100 or 500 miles of fence and you are only putting up

2 miles. They may charge 50 miles but not keep livestock in for more than the first few hundred yards.

Think of chargers like pickup trucks. If you had a half-ton pickup with a 6-cylinder motor, it might pull your loaded stock trailer slowly down the road if it was downhill or flat, or not loaded. But, that is rarely the case. When you encounter hills or want to go faster to pass someone, or fill the trailer full, you need a 1-ton pickup with more horsepower. Both pickups will pull the trailer — only one of them would you take on a long cross-country haul. You should buy chargers by the output joules rating that you can count on for the long haul.

If you can use a 110-volt AC charger it will be cheaper and more reliable than a 12-volt battery charger. We have run wire down the side of a road and under two bridges in order to use a plug in charger in a 110 outlet when there was no electricity at the pasture. A 5-joule charger and solar panel will cost you as much as a 20-joule AC charger. You don't necessarily need a solar panel but it makes things more trouble free. A 5-joule charger will run down a 12-volt battery in about a week with no solar panel. With a solar panel to charge the battery it will run trouble free for years.

> *You should buy chargers by the output joules rating that you can count on for the long haul.*

We have some with and some without solar panels and I guess the goats stay in at both places so that is all that matters. Although I will forget to take a new battery to the non-solar panel charger on occasion and it will go dead for a few days, the goats don't seem to find out. For a solar panel and DC charger, I like the Taylor Fencing set up. Again, be creative and if at all possible use an AC charger.

I feel it is best to use 12.5-gauge high tensile wire. It is tough and carries the electricity further with less resistance than 14-gauge. Don't use polywire on permanent fencing. It doesn't carry the electricity on a stretch of fence over a quarter of a mile very well. I don't use it, except in gates or water gap drop wires, or if I am running a temporary fence, such as strip grazing.

I would also say that you shouldn't expect electric fencing to work in an area that you are pushing or pressuring the goats through, as in a corral or alleyway. These can be made with wire cattle panels or 6 x 12 woven wire, and steel "T" post.

> *It may go without saying but the best way to keep goats from getting out is to not let them get hungry.*

It may go without saying but the best way to keep goats from getting out is to not let them get hungry. If the hunger pains are greater than the pain of the electric fence, they will choose the lesser pain every time. I've had people call me about not being able to keep their goats in. I ask them how much forage the goats have to eat in the pasture. They tell me they have plenty to eat. I ask them to take a grocery sack and go out in your pasture and pull good green forage and put it in the grocery sack until it is full. Don't fill it with dried grass and sticks. Then call me back and tell me how long that takes you. This is how much every doe in your pasture needs to eat, every day of the year. If you have 100 does in a pasture that is 100 sacks of grass, weeds or browse every day. If during the dry months of August you couldn't fill one sack per goat on your pasture, your goats will look for a place to get something to eat. If during the winter they don't have enough hay or other forage, your goats will look for a place to get it. Sure, there are a few goats that seem to want to be fence jumpers and they need to be eliminated, but if you constantly have goats that are getting out I usually tell people that they are just hungry and until you fix that problem they will continue to find a way to get out.

A good ground for your electric fence is very important. Your charger should come with instructions on how many ground rods to use and how to space them according to the joule output of the charger you have purchased. Occasionally, during dry weather, you may be feeling that your charger isn't putting out as much voltage as it used to, but there is no short in it. You may need to soak the area of your ground rods with water. This will take more than a bucket or two, maybe a hundred gallons or more. I have not experienced this problem but I've been aware of it. We usually experience a month of hot, very dry summer weather, but having multiple ground rods driven 5-6 feet deep helps alleviate this problem.

Having snow or ice on your wires during the winter is another issue you will deal with in some climates. I have not had animals getting out during the winter. Usually it is for two reasons. They have adequate hay in their pasture and they are so used to the electric wire they won't go near it. It will still shock them through the snow, although, with them standing on the snow, they will be somewhat insulated from the electric shock and may not get a full charge. This is yet another reason to have a more powerful charger. When the snow or ice starts to melt it may short out your charger for a while. A strong charger will still have some voltage left at the end of the fence. I rarely have any problems, because the goats have learned to stay away from the fence.

I occasionally have a pasture of goats that continue to get out until I figure out the problem.

There are a few things different about goats when they get out of a pasture than what you may be used to with cattle.

Goats will usually stay very close to the pasture they've gotten out of. They are slow to venture out into unknown territory, probably because they know they are prey and won't quickly move into unfamiliar areas. When you turn a group of cows into a new pasture the first thing they do is to walk around the fence line looking for a place to escape. The first day you take goats to a new pasture, they will only go a few hundred yards from the place where you let them out of the trailer. The next day they will only be a few hundred yards farther. It may take them several days to move around the whole pasture.

If you bring home a few head of goats you've bought, you need to keep them in a very secure goat-proof corral for a few days. If they get out in the first few days after they are in their new surroundings they will often run several miles looking for other goats. I have heard of them going 8-10 miles or more. After they have been on your place for a few days they will settle in and call it home.

If you have one or two that slip through the wire and are in the road ditch, usually a car going by the road will scare them back where they belong. After goats are in a pasture for a few weeks they know where they belong and are easy to get back in if they do get out.

When you come upon a group of goats that have gotten out of your pasture and you are trying to put them back in, you can actually have them show you where they got out. First off, do not grab a bucket of feed and lead them towards the gate and back into the pasture. You need to make them think they are in danger. The way I do this is to get my dog out and drive them away from me and toward their pasture. I don't let the dog chase them too hard and make them panic and make another hole in the fence. You want them to walk back into the pasture where they were safe, but pressure them only to the extent that they go back to the place they got out. Follow them with light pressure pushing towards the fence but letting them choose which way they go once they're at the fence line. With a little patience and the right amount of pressure applied to the goats, they will lead you back to where they got out, going back in through the same spot in the fence. Then you can fix the fence problem.

Recently I have had a group of goats that kept getting out into a soybean field next to their pasture. When I would apply this technique they would run to a certain place in the fence and stand, wanting to get back to their pasture but acting like they were not able to get in. Then they would go to another spot in the fence and do the same thing. After looking closely I discovered that they were climbing up some trees that were leaning across the fence and jumping off to the other side. They weren't able to jump back up to the tree to climb back over.

If you don't have a herding dog you can easily drive goats by cracking a bullwhip or even just clapping your hands loudly. This is an effective way to move them in a corral or alleyway.

CHAPTER 7

KEEPING 'EM ALIVE

Goats provide some health challenges that, if you are a cattle producer, you may not have seen before. This chapter isn't a full list of diseases and treatments for goats. There are many good books written by expert veterinarians full of diseases and diagnosis for goats and sheep. I would highly recommend you purchase "Sheep and Goat Medicine", by D.G. Pugh, DVM. It may be expensive but one goat problem and you will soon have a huge return on that investment.

You will also need a good working relationship with a veterinarian that will learn about pasture goats if he doesn't already have some experience in that area. Most antibiotics, prescription and over the counter, and dewormers are not labeled for goats and must be prescribed by a veterinarian.

It is not legal or ethical for me or any other goat producer who is not a licensed veterinarian to recommend drugs that are not labeled for goats. For that reason, I will purposely be very vague concerning any treatments that I use.

The following diseases and problems are simply a list of ones that I have encountered, so you probably will too.

Pinkeye

When you are buying does to start your herd, you will undoubtedly have some that will turn up blind after you've had them a week or two. Sometimes this just happens in one eye, which is not as troublesome as when they get it in both.

The eye will become cloudy and maybe matted with mucus around the edge. This seems to happen to some goats when they are stressed and from what research I have done I believe it is Chlamydia that is causing the eye problems. If they have it only in one eye, they can still eat and find water, I usually treat them with an antibiotic and may spray a cattle "pink eye" type spray in both eyes. If they have it in both eyes it is a good idea to put them in a smaller pen for a few days where they can find water and feed. They will usually get over it in a week or so, and will get their eyesight back. If you treat them they may get over it slightly sooner or they may not. Truthfully, there doesn't seem to be a very effective treatment. The stress it causes can also cause pneumonia, or hinder their resistance to a worm load.

Abortions

In the early years of our goat business I had several does aborting kids during the last few weeks of pregnancy. This is often caused by a different strain of Chlamydia. There are other diseases that can also cause late-term abortions but the treatment is usually the same. We may have had 30-50% of our does abort that year. That was another year I almost sold out. We now may have an occasional abortion in first time kidders but nothing to that magnitude has happened since. I didn't get rid of these goats; we were trying desperately to build our herd then and there were enough other things to cull goats out of the herd for, so if I did, I soon wouldn't have had any goats on the place.

There's no practical way to tell if a goat has Chlamydia before you buy them and I believe most goats have been exposed to it. Once they have an abortion due to Chlamydia they seem to build immunity to it from then on, carrying their pregnancy to full term in the following years. It is best to buy does from a producer who has been in business for several years. These does will have some natural immunity to this and other abortion type diseases due to the fact that they would put the producer out of business if they didn't.

You simply can't tell if you are going to have this problem until you start having abortions. At that point you should consult your veterinarian. You may ask them about preventative measures to take but as far as I know, there is nothing labeled for this kind of use in goats and no vaccine available. I've never known anyone else to have a problem of the magnitude I experienced so I just chalk it up to bad luck and I wouldn't let it worry you.

By having does giving birth in open pasture and not in crowded pens will also keep this from spreading.

Floppy Kid Syndrome
During our first kidding season I had a terrible experience that almost made me want to quit before we ever raised our first kid crop. I would have kids born and doing fine for about a week then they would become weak and not be able to stand.

First I would notice them being somewhat uncoordinated, walking but staggering ever so slightly. They would soon become limp, without any muscle tone, like a wet noodle. I contacted other goat producers and veterinarians in Kansas, Missouri, Oklahoma and Texas. I sent kids for a necropsy, trying to find out what was causing this. It started in just a few kids that were born, but soon it was happening to every kid born when they were 7-10 days old. Finally, after exhausting all other possibilities, I was convinced it was Floppy Kid Syndrome.

The kids had all the symptoms and there seems to be no real diagnostic test for it, or cause, or even a good treatment. It has something to do with the mother's milk and bacteria that gets started in the stomach of the kid. I tried all available antibiotic treatment, some by injection, and some orally, along with Pepto-Bismol, Baking Soda and water, vegetable oil. Everyone I talked to had something to try and I would think that it was working but the outcome was usually the same. I was losing kids as fast as they were being born.

I was finally able to come up with a way to keep them alive until the problem could run its course. As soon as I would notice them slightly uncoordinated in their walking, or even walking slowly when they should have been running, I would use 45 cc of Lactated Ringers and 15 cc of Dextrose solution, injecting it under the skin in the shoulder of the kid, tubing 30 cc of vegetable oil into their stomach and 1 cc of an oral antibiotic. This would sometimes keep them alive until they were strong enough to tube milk down them.

> *I found that catching them early was the key to making the treatment successful.*

Depending on how early in the problem I spotted them and started the treatment, I might have to keep this up several times a day, for a few days. I found that catching them early was the key to making the treatment successful. Being new into goats I wasn't prepared with adequate pen space for each doe and kid that I had to bring in and treat for several days, so I had to take a few off their mothers to treat them regularly. Some does wouldn't accept their kids back if I was able to get them up on their feet, so we had a lot of bottle kids that year. I noticed more of my kids from my Boer bucks were having this problem. I suspect they were nursing more because they were bigger at a week of age than my Spanish-cross kids.

I was told this problem hits all goat producers to some degree or another sometime during their years in the business, but usually only to one or two kids and you simply find them dead or very limp and lifeless and never know what the problem was. Luckily at that time I only had about 100 does. I had them all in one pasture by my house to watch more closely.

That was our first year kidding goats and probably our worst year ever. You will probably never experience this to the degree that it occurred for me, as I have never talked to any other goat producer that has.

Pneumonia

Although I vaccinate for Pneumonia, using a vaccine made by Colorado Serum that is labeled for goats, I will still have a few Pneumonia problems occasionally. You should consult your veterinarian for the best antibiotic treatment. There are few antibiotics labeled for goats but you can use some cattle antibiotics under your veterinarian's recommendations. No matter what you treat pneumonia with; the most important thing is to catch it early. Goats don't seem to want you to know they are sick until they are very sick. This is especially true of the smaller weaned goats you are growing post weaning. You will also want to deworm them again if you are treating for pneumonia as any stress on the animal will make them less able to handle any parasite load.

> *Goats don't seem to want you to know they are sick until they are very sick.*

The symptoms are the same as in cattle respiratory diseases: listlessness, not eating, mucus discharge around the nose and labored breathing. Concerning a goat, you need to carefully look at any goat that is not with the herd, or who is lying down when everyone else is up and grazing. If the dog is lying next to him you should be particularly suspicious. The LGDs spend their whole life with the goats and will know before you do if one is having a problem.

Sore Mouth

I will occasionally have a few kids get Sore Mouth. They will have wart-like growths around their mouth. It usually happens in young kids before weaning. It can be transmitted to the mother's udder, which makes it very uncomfortable for the kid to nurse, and she may kick him away. I have never had this happen that I know of and I don't believe I have ever lost a kid to Sore Mouth. It is more cosmetic than life threatening and I don't treat infected kids or isolate them. They seem to get over it in a few weeks and do just fine.

There is a vaccine for this, but for commercial goat producers I wouldn't think you would want to vaccinate against it. I have also been told you can spray WD 40 on the sores and they will heal quicker. You might want to treat one if he is going to be shown in the fair or taken to a buck test, or you will soon have him mingling with someone else's goats.

I have heard that it can be transmitted to humans if you are handling goats with Sore Mouth, but I have never had that happen either.

Broken Leg

If you have goats for long you will probably experience a broken leg or two from a goat trying to jump a fence or any number of unknown causes. One year in one particular pasture we had 6 broken legs in a two-week period and never did find out the cause of it.

I have been very successful splinting the leg with a piece of PVC pipe. Take a 1 1/2-inch piece of pipe about 8 inches long and split it lengthwise with a saw. Now take the two halves and place it along the length of the broken leg and tape it with duct tape, wrapping it up on the leg to keep it from sliding down. You will want to leave it on for about 6 weeks. If this is during hot weather when flies are bad you will want to keep fly spray on it so maggots won't get in.

Almost any break on one of the long bones of a front or back leg can be splinted successfully this way, unless it is a compound fracture with the bone sticking out. In that case my experience is that it is best to euthanize the animal.

Abscesses, Caseous Lymphadenitis, CL

If you have goats for any length of time, you will have some that get an abscess behind their ear or jaw. These may or may not be CL abscesses. This seems to happen to most goats and in my opinion is not a big problem as far as their ability to produce. It is not life threatening and you can lance it or stick a needle in it and drain it, or simply let it burst on its own. It will heal just the same and you will have a scar in the area of the abscess.

Not that CL could not kill a goat if they got abscesses around their vital organs, but as far as I know, I've never had a goat die from that, but I have had goats die for unexplainable reasons, so that could have been one of the reasons.

When you are buying goats you will probably get them home and notice that many have these scars. It has never kept one of my goats from being a good producer.

Coccidiosis

The only time I have a goat with persistent diarrhea is from stomach worms or coccidiosis. Along with parasites, coccidiosis seems to be one the biggest problem I experience with weaned kids.

> *The only time I have a goat with persistent diarrhea is from stomach worms or coccidiosis.*

I have read that the organism is always present but when kids are under stressful conditions their resistance and tolerance to it is much lower and it becomes a problem. I use Rumensin in my feed for a coccidiostat. It helps to prevent coccidiosis but is not a cure. I will still have some cases as the ones that are stressed more won't eat and they are the problems.

It is important to keep them hydrated. Drenching with electrolytes is one therapy. I have tried different methods but it all seems to stress the goat more. There is no labeled treatment for coccidiosis in goats so again you will need to consult your local veterinarian for more recommendations.

Sometimes it seems the more extreme measures I use to cure him the faster he dies. I often feel like leaving them in the pasture and administering medications there is less stressful for the goat and enhances the chance of recovery. My record of success is about the same whether I put a goat in a sick pen or leave them in the pasture after medicating them. If it is a multi-day coccidiosis treatment I will bring him to a small pen for my own convenience.

Parasites, coccidiosis and pneumonia, in that order, are the three biggest killers of my weaned goats. I have only limited success at curing any goats that come down with an acute case of any one of these three and some come down with all three at once when one of them stresses their body. I feel like whatever can be done to create a less stressful environment at weaning is probably worth the investment.

I try to get them to eat a 16% pelleted feed that is very palatable as quick as I can. But I also want to turn them out on good pasture. I've had bad experience with keeping them in a dry lot situation even though I was feeding good hay. These kids have never seen hay before and it is always less palatable than the forage they were used to while with their mothers. They will eat some but they probably won't have the feed intake they need to provide adequate nutrition to fight off the stress of this time.

I will have some does that I am culling out from the same herds these kids came from. I will put them with the weaned kids and they will be fed together. These does know what a feed bucket is. By having them in the herd of freshly weaned kids, most the kids will follow them and start eating with the does. I'll feed them .25 - .5lb. / hd. / day while they are under stress of weaning. I will pour the feed on the ground in piles about 10 feet apart. This lets me spread a bucket of feed out in eight or ten piles, allowing more goats to get next to the feed. It also lets me move their feeding area every day. Feed troughs may be better; they must be short in height for these kids. They will always jump in them if they can, pooping and walking through them. It seems that for me, putting it on the ground in a new spot every day is the option I am going with until I am convinced of a better way for us. By putting it in piles instead of stringing the feed out along the ground, the goats will be more likely to not be walking and pooping on it as their heads are down eating and tails out of the feed.

After they are mostly doing well I may stop feeding them as much or do it every other day until I want to get them up to full feed in November. I believe nutrition is the key to keeping these goats able to handle the stress of weaning. The female kids that I leave on their mothers don't have the weaning stress and never have as many problems as those fresh weaned buck kids. Maybe someday I will figure out a better way.

Other diseases common to goats

Mastitis, Clostridium Perfringens, Tetanus, Pregnancy Toxemia, Goat Polio and White Muscle Disease are some other diseases that you as a goat producer should be aware of. I will only mention them here as I have not personally experienced them, at least to my knowledge. You will sometimes find a goat dead that you thought was perfectly healthy the day before, so unless you necropsy every death you may never really know. Of course if you begin to have several problems with the same symptoms you will want to consult your veterinarian. Again I will recommend buying "Sheep and Goat Medicine", by Dr. Pugh; you might want to give a copy to your veterinarian for Christmas if he doesn't have one.

Other ways to kill goats

Just between you and me, goat diseases are not the only thing that may kill my goats. Sometimes there are strange things that can happen to goats during their lifetime.

I thought I should include a section on how I have killed goats, or at least seen them die, or been lucky enough to rescue them from, "just in time". Maybe if you are made aware of these problems, you can head them off before they occur. But many of them are just "things that happen to goats."

I've had goats get their head stuck in the fork of a tree. One goat was up very high into the tree, it must have climbed up then gotten stuck. I couldn't climb up and get him so I cut the tree down and saved him before he died. I've lost goats that got their head stuck in the pen that surrounds our dog food feeders, and in old woven wire fence that was torn down and rolled up, then thrown in a ditch.

I lost six does, some kids and a couple bucks that were hit by lightning under a tree.

One summer it was very hot and dry and I had a small kid that got stuck in a crack in the ground and then dehydrated and died.

I have lost more than one goat that has gotten stuck in the mud around a pond. I thought a water tank would be the best way to water them, but I have had them drown in a water tank, also. It is a good idea to get some cement blocks and make steps inside the tank so they can get out.

I will occasionally have a goat have an allergic reaction to a vaccine, which sends them into respiratory distress.

I was hauling about 75 fat goats to a sale and had six dead when I got there because they piled up and some got suffocated. No one told me you should always "gate" goats in a trailer.

I've had them suffocate and die after they piled on one another in a barn during a storm. I like having shelter for them but no matter how big the barn, they may all crowd into one corner. Thankfully it only happens occasionally, but can happen with the kids during rain or snow that sometimes occurs in the spring kidding season.

I have had them get stuck in the mineral feeder and die.

I have not found a hay feeder that I can be confident that the bale won't fall over on them as they eat around the bottom. I have tried several but none are foolproof. I've lost several due to that happening. If you put a large round bale out you may want to set it so the strings are going around the bale horizontally, and the flat ends are up and down. Although this will allow rain to soak into the hay and rot or mold much quicker, it may keep the bale from falling on them, but you should still beware. You should push it over before it falls if the goats are eating the bottom out from under it and it resembles a huge mushroom.

I have accidentally run over them with my pickup. I used to honk to get them out of the way but once I had one of my expensive Myotonic bucks (fainting goats) fall over when I honked and then I felt a tire run up and over him. He fainted for a long time after that.

I've had a guard dog that went psycho and began killing my goats.

> *they sometimes die for no good reason. That's just part of the business you have to deal with so don't take it personal.*

All these are just the ways I have found up to now that goats die. I am sure by the time I am done with this book I could add some more to this list, and along with the normal parasites and disease issues, they sometimes die for no good reason. That's just part of the business you have to deal with so don't take it personal.

CHAPTER 8

CO-GRAZING GOATS AND CATTLE

I have pastures with only goats, some with only cattle and some with goats and cattle. They get along fine. The guard dogs get used to the cattle being there, although the goats and cattle rarely graze close together. The cattle prefer grass but I do see them eating tree leaves occasionally. The goats prefer trees and brush but I do see them eating grass sometimes.

I've been told that you can add one to two does for every cow you have in your pasture and not change the stocking rate of your cattle. There really is no good rule of thumb to stocking a pasture with goats and cows. Your stocking rate will vary depending on how much area is brush and weeds that the cows are not utilizing. I have a pasture of 80 acres that I would put 16 cows on from April 15 – Nov. 15 before I had goats. Then I put 150 goats on it year-round with no cattle for a few years. Before the goats were brought in, this pasture had small Cedar trees and Buckbrush all over it,

> **In about three years of goats and no mowing, the Cedars, Buckbrush, Ragweed and Thistles were gone.**

along with Ragweed and Musk Thistle. It needed mowing every year just to keep it from getting worse. In about three years of goats and no mowing, the Cedars, Buckbrush, Ragweed and Thistles were gone. I have since put 10 cows and calves back in the pasture and keep about 100 does and their kids there.

It is more work to have cattle and goats in the same pasture as you may need dual facilities for handling each one, and it is less efficient use of guard dogs to guard a fewer number of goats in the same pasture, but I feel I have less parasite problems. Stomach worms from a goat cannot live in the environment of a cattle stomach, and stomach worms from cattle cannot live in the environment of a goat stomach. The cattle will eat and mop up the goat parasites and the goats do the same for the cattle.

A neighbor asked me if I would bring goats to his pasture. He was mowing it every year just to stay ahead of the locust and hedge sprouts. It is 160 acres and he runs 40 cows and calves there year round. The first year I put in 120 does and their kids and I have decreased the goats to about 60 does that stay there all year. I put up the one wire electric fence around the perimeter of the pasture. He no longer mows the pasture, the Ragweed, Buckbrush and Sprouts are on their way to being eliminated and he no longer gets calls of his cattle being out with my electric fence inside the perimeter of the cow fence.

Last year I fenced and put 50 does and kids on 50 acres of Locust and Hedge sprouts, Ragweed and Thistles. This pasture was an eyesore. It was completely eaten down by overgrazing and was covered with thistles. I saw only two thistles this year that the goats missed and I had to take care of. The Ragweed is smaller but still there. The Buckbrush is gone and the sprouts are about half gone. Of course to get good control of sprouts they should be small so the goats can get at least most of them defoliated. The goats will stand on their hind legs to reach up and graze. They also will consume the bark at some times of the year and kill them

In pastures where I have goats all year I have very few Thistles, Cedars, Buckbrush, Tree sprouts, or Ragweed.

out that way. In pastures where I have goats all year I have very few Thistles, Cedars, Buckbrush, Tree sprouts, or Ragweed.

Sericea lespedeza has become a problem in this area of the Midwest. It has been declared by Kansas and other states as a Noxious Weed and landowners are required by law to control it. This is mostly done by spraying, which is not only expensive and time consuming but it has very limited long-term effectiveness. I have never seen anyone who had it start in their pasture able to totally get rid of it or even keep it from spreading. Cattle won't eat Sericea so it can totally ruin cattle grazing by crowding out other forbs and grasses.

Goats love to eat Sericea Lespedeza. I have none in the pastures where there are goats. I remember the year when hay was in short supply and expensive. I bought some hay and while feeding it I realized then why nobody else had bought it. It was infested with Sericea and the seed. I ended up feeding it on my own place. I have not spotted a single Sericea plant in the eight years since.

I know a goat producer who took his children and gathered Sericea seeds off of a nearby CRP field. He spread it on his pastures and got it established, but he has to rotate the goats off of it or they will kill it out.

There are also studies that show the tannins in some plants actually are natural dewormers for goats. Two plants that are high in tannins are Sericea Lespedeza and Cedar trees.

I am currently fencing 240 acres of pasture on which the owner has cattle. The Sericea is winning the battle and taking over the pasture. The pasture also has a lot of small sprouts that came up from broken off roots after the owner pushed some trees out with a bulldozer. He is glad to have my goats coming in next spring after seeing other pastures on which I graze. I am glad to have the Sericea and other brush and weeds for goat pasture. It takes more management and "public relations" on my part. I need to monitor the grazing so as to not over graze with goats and force them to eat more grass that the cattle will need. My goats will do well there and I would be surprised if they didn't wean the heaviest kids of any of my pastures.

I don't know how to put a value on the brush and weed control I get from my goats but the county average price for mowing pasture is over \$15/acre or it would cost over \$20/acre to spray it and the effectiveness of those methods is questionable and would need to be done yearly.

There is not that much to say about this concept except that it works. Cattlemen can use goats to make a better cattle pasture, and if you've only had goats on a pasture for a few years you can put cattle on it and wait for the brush and weeds to come back and make a better goat pasture. You can put both species on the pasture together to maximize the forage available.

CHAPTER 9

FEEDING THE BREEDING HERD
THROUGH THE WINTER

Some people ask me if you have to feed a goat through the winter.

In my pastures the goats will stay there all year long. I will stock the pasture with the intent to have some grass left over in the fall that will help supplement them through the winter. That being the case, I will usually take some hay to them starting in January and feeding through most of March and part of April. This depends on how much pasture forage is available. My pickup has a hay-feeding type bed that unrolls the hay. When they eat it all I will take them more, as long as they clean it up.

My goats do not like fescue hay and will only eat our native grass hay slightly better if it has forbs or weeds in it. They like brome, lespedeza, clovers, even rag weeds and other broad leaf weeds rolled into a bale. They won't eat the heavy stems of Giant

Ragweeds very well but will consume the leafy vegetation. Your goats may learn to eat whatever hay you have available, although they may not consume as much of it as they would if they were to like it better.

To me, the more they eat, the better they will do. I have been called to look at goats that had plenty of hay in front of them but were very skinny. The first thing I do is check their eyelids for anemia caused by parasites. Then I look at the type of hay they are eating. If it is stemmy and coarse, as in over-mature native blue stem pasture grass, or over-mature fescue, they will not eat much of it and they also can't cope with any type of parasite load if they are nutritionally starving. A goat cannot physically consume enough hay in the 4%-5% protein range to keep them in good shape. They only have so much capacity to digest forage.

> *A goat cannot physically consume enough hay in the 4%-5% protein range to keep them in good shape.*

I figure my does will eat about 4 lbs. of forage a day. As the grass gets picked over through the winter, they may go out and browse 1 lb. of that and then eat 3 lbs. of hay a day. They will consume less hay early in the winter feeding month of January, then more as the winter progresses. Of course they will eat less as the grass begins to come on in the spring again. When there is snow on the ground I have seen my goats and cattle dig through the snow and graze standing fescue. I usually like to take some hay out to them in snowy weather though; maybe I just think it is what I should do or feel sorry for them. I figure in bad weather the more they eat the better they will cope with it and the less energy they must use to go out and find a meal. They probably wouldn't starve to death without the hay but they won't have to dig through the snow.

By lowering my stocking density and leaving some standing forage for the fall and winter, it makes my winter-feeding load much less burdensome. I especially want to do this on pastures that are several miles away.

Many people complain about goats wasting a lot of hay. I'm not sure that they waste any more than cattle do if they were treated the same way. They will waste less hay if the hay is of good quality. They will waste less hay if they are not allowed to walk and poop all over it. They will waste less hay if they are only given enough for one or two days at a time. The same goes with cattle, horses or elephants. It is just a little harder to accomplish with goats.

I will unroll what I consider one day's worth of hay in the area I want to feed the goats that day. Then I might go to another area of the pasture, preferably where they can't see me, and while they are eating I will unroll another day's worth of hay at the other location. After they eat their fill and are hungry again, they will forage around the pasture and find the other hay left the day before. Depending on the price of hay and the cost involved with feeding it, I will probably let them waste some hay instead of coming back daily to feed. If goats have feed and water and are not kidding or having any other problems or reasons for me to check them more regular, I may only check them once a week or whenever I need to take dog food to the self-feeders.

Do you feed grain or sack feed?

I've had people ask me if I feed "sacked grain" as if this means that your goats are superior if you do not feed them grain or feed from a sack.

> *I will feed them whatever is most economical for the nutrition they need during the year, depending on the forage that they have available and the time and labor I have available.*

I will feed them whatever is most economical for the nutrition they need during the year, depending on the forage that they have available and the time and labor I have available. If there is a drought and fall forage is limited I will supplement them with hay earlier in the year or other protein and energy supplements.

I have fed Dried Distillers Grain (DDG) feed by-products from our local ethanol plant. It is probably the most economical much of the time but is more labor intensive and time consuming to feed. I get it in bulk and take it out in buckets, feeding it on the ground in piles. I know feeding on the ground may not be the best method but I can move feeding sites every day and under normal conditions they do not waste very much. You can also buy it in a sack; you will just pay about $2 per hundredweight more for the bagging. Some people feed whole corn and that is OK, too. Corn has 8% - 9% protein. DDG has about 25% protein and as much energy as corn, so I prefer that even if corn is a little cheaper. You should figure the price you're paying for feed against the nutritional value and time and labor involved in feeding. If you have cattle or other livestock, whatever supplement you are feeding them will most likely work for goats.

Last year I didn't need to feed any protein supplements until about 30 days prior to kidding and 30 days after kidding, which in my case was mid-February to mid-April. This is the time of the does' highest nutritional needs, so unless you have abundant high-quality forage for them, you will need to supplement during this stage of production.

I used a 200-lb. protein tub during this time. During kidding season, I do not like the does to come running towards me as I enter the pasture, leaving their kids behind, thinking that I'm bringing them something to eat, as in DDG, corn, etc. By having the tubs out 24/7 during this time, they will usually stay with their kids so you can look them over if you're not bringing them something tasty every day. These protein tubs cost me almost twice as much as the same protein and mineral supplement I could buy in the bulk and take out and feed by hand, but the extra labor and fuel cost more than the savings on the feed. The "no sack feed" producers often do not realize that feed tubs are sack feed in a tub, protein blocks are sack feed in a block form, range cubes are sack feed made into a cube, alfalfa is also another form of sack feed that is grown and put into a bale. There is no reason not to feed sack feed if your goats need the nutrition and it is the most economical or effective way for you to feed them, based upon the time you have available and the facilities you have to handle feed supplements. You may want to feed more grain and less hay if grain is cheap and hay is scarce. I have done this in some years. You just need to have a

> *The market doesn't care how much it cost you to raise your goat. It's worth is based on what someone is willing to pay to put it on their plate.*

good reason for every dollar you put into your livestock. The market doesn't care how much it cost you to raise your goat. It's worth is based on what someone is willing to pay to put it on their plate.

Do you feed a special "goat" mineral?

I keep free choice mineral out for my goats just as you would to any livestock. There is usually nothing magical or specific to goat mineral that is labeled as such at your local feed store, except the price tag. My goats will eat the same mineral supplement that my cattle eat.

Some people believe goats cannot be fed copper but this is not true. Some sheep shouldn't be supplemented copper in various areas of the Midwest due to the copper level in the soils and the vegetation, and the fact that sheep store more copper in their liver. If you feed a Sheep and Goat mineral, it likely will be formulated for sheep and not have enough copper in it for goats.

I like to feed a mineral with the high amount of copper, 2000 ppm – 3000 ppm. The general consensus is that it helps with the anemia that they might suffer from while carrying a high parasite load. If you have a mineral that you are satisfied with for your other livestock and it is economically priced, I would use it for my goats, also. You can compare the feed tag of goat mineral versus cattle mineral and compare that to the price.

You should learn how to use the "goat nutrient calculator", available online at Langston University's website, at www.luresext. edu. There you can put in your own values for hay that you've had tested and are feeding, or use the standard values for your type hay that is available. You can then plug in the supplements you have available and find out the lowest cost ration based on your prices. I use this for winter feeding my doe herd as well as growing my weaned kids.

CHAPTER 10

FEEDING THE KIDS FROM WEANING TO MARKET

I will wean my kids in late July or August because the buck kids will begin to breed the mature nannies that are starting to cycle by this time. If you castrate your kids you wouldn't necessarily have to wean this early.

At weaning I will deworm the does and kids. The kids will get CDT and pneumonia vaccines at that time. The does and replacement doelings that I want to keep will go back to pasture.

I have started leaving my nanny replacement kids on their mothers, letting them wean themselves. I like this practice because I don't have a separate place to put my nanny kids to keep the buck kids from trying to breed them while I am feeding them out for market. I'll put my breeding bucks with my mature nannies in the fall. The replacement doelings will still be in the pasture with their mothers; they will have weaned themselves by that time. Some will breed that first year, some will not, depending on their size. I usually just plan on breeding the doelings to kid as 2-year-olds, but if some breed and kid as 1-year-olds it is usually not a problem. I will sort off those that are "making a bag" in March when I am doing the CDT and pneumonia revaccinations and deworming. I'll put them in a pasture closer to home where I'll see them more often during kidding.

> **Sometimes you get lucky, just don't build your whole operation around it.**

That being said, I had a pasture where I put the other replacement doelings, the ones that were not making a bag by March. I wasn't checking them much while the other does were kidding. When I did get there to check them I had more than 20 kids on the ground and doing fine. Sometimes you get lucky, just don't build your whole operation around it.

The buck kids and other doelings will be penned for several days after weaning and fed a feed mix that is made up of DDG, corn and vitamins and minerals, running 16%-20% protein, depending on feed cost, and the hay I have available. This is a good time to add a coccidiostat, also. I will feed them in the pen until they are coming to feed and then follow me out the gate. The ones that don't follow will stay in the pen until they are coming to feed.

These kids will average 35 lbs. - 45 lbs. I know some producers tell me they wean 50 - 60 lb. kids or bigger but that's not what mine average in August.

I will feed them 1/3 - 1/2 lb. feed mix / hd. / day while they are in the pen. Their total feed intake will be less than 2 lb. dry matter / hd. / day. They go into a pasture that was cut for hay in June and then allowed to grow back. Cutting it for hay helps to eliminate many of the parasites on this pasture and makes the grass and clovers more palatable. I want the weanlings to have the best of what I have available. The better quality feed they have available encourages them to eat more and increases their plane of nutrition so they are better able to handle stress and survive. Changing any goats' environment causes them stress. When you have to change their environment, increasing their level of nutrition will help them make the transition with fewer problems.

During the course of two weeks we will be gathering several different pastures to wean kids. It would be much easier if they were all in one larger pasture but that's not the way it is for us. A couple weeks after the last pasture is gathered I will revaccinate all the kids that have been moved home with the CDT and pneumonia vaccine and I will check their eyes for anemia using the FAMACHA technique, and deworm accordingly, knowing that they have just been dewormed a few weeks ago.

These kids are very vulnerable to parasites and coccidiosis at this time. I'll pull a few kids that have diarrhea and put them in a sick pen, drenching them with a coccidiostat and adding it to the water. We have found that it is a good idea to sell any kids that are very small and not doing well at this time or before. We call them the "Dinks". They are the "dinky" goats. They will always be Dinks. They won't bring much money but they never will and most of them will die before they get on the truck to go to market with the rest. If they don't die, they will be sorted off by the buyer and you'll not get much for them later — after they've eaten feed for a few months. They are usually dinks because they are more susceptible to worms and will be worm factories, contaminating the pasture for the other weaned kids. Just take them to the closest goat auction and leave them. Don't watch them sell. Just go home and forget about them. Take my word on this; anything you get for them is better than what they are worth when you are hauling them to the dead pile.

> *Changing any goats' environment causes them stress.*

My biggest death loss seems to be post weaning. It has ranged up to 12%. This is an area that I would like to drastically improve. If you sell the dinks you will probably cut this in half. I have talked to some who buy feeder goats and they will figure at least 10% death loss and they are very picky about what they buy. Usually the health problems during this time are parasites, coccidiosis and pneumonia. The first few weeks are not necessarily the worst. Some problem kids can slip up on you long after you have most of them straightened out.

Any kid that has diarrhea will need to be treated. Unless his eyelids are bright red, I will usually deworm him again and then treat for coccidiosis. This is the time of year that I will use my microscope to determine if I have coccidiosis or a stomach worm problem. It is easy to see in a fecal sample. But honestly, in these fresh weaned kids, if they have diarrhea they will normally have coccidiosis and a parasite load, so you may as well treat them for both.

At this point, if their pasture is good I may not feed them daily. You can also dry lot these meat kids and save your pastures for the breeding does. You may need to feed them grain daily if they are eating hay that is in the 6% -10% protein range. It depends upon your marketing plan. I have been asked about implanting the kids with a growth implant like those used for cattle. I'm sure there is not an implant available that is labeled for goats.

Up until this year I have fed these goats by hand with feed buckets but carrying more than 40,000 lbs. of feed in buckets has made me change my strategy. In the past I used the same DDG feed mix as I previously described and started to feed them daily in November as the forage quality declined. I will increase their mixed feed to 2 lbs. / hd. / day as I feed to market weight. You may need to limit their hay intake to get them to eat more grain. It seems as though a goat just likes to browse and will go out and pick at winter pasture that doesn't have much nutritional value rather than eat another ½ lb. of grain. That extra grain intake is the key to feeding goats or any animal. There is a certain amount of calories that are used to just maintain an animal; every bite he takes after maintenance requirements are met is going toward weight gain. The more they eat, the more they gain and also the more efficiently they gain.

> *The more they eat, the more they gain and also the more efficiently they gain.*

When they are eating all that I give to them and leaving a little on the ground, I will take out a self-feeder with the same feed mix in it to eliminate the handling of so many buckets.

I'm not sure how well I like feeding with the self-feeder yet. I am still evaluating that method. When you feed by hand you can see if all the goats are coming up to eat. You can easily notice if a sick goat is not eating, and you also have a good handle on their overall feed intake. I haven't come up with a simpler or better method to feed these goats to market weight other than to bucket feed them by hand or have a cube feeder on my pickup that delivers the feed on the ground or in a feed bunk that you would have to clean out every day. With a pickup truck feeder feeding on the ground, you would have to drive very quickly to not run over anybody.

How economical is it to feed out your weaned goats?

Some people say that you can't make money feeding a goat. I say that if you keep them alive and keep them eating, most years you should be able to make money, but there are no guarantees in life. When I wean my goats they may only weigh 40 lbs. This past year a 40 lb. feeder goat is worth about $1.25 in August when I wean them. A 50 lb. goat may be worth $1.50. The market is usually at its lowest in June, July, August, and starts to move up slowly in Oct., Nov. and Dec. It may peak during the Jan., Feb., March time frame. This cycle has gone on for as long as I've watched the goat market, more than 12 years, and doesn't seem to have all that much to do with Muslim holidays, as I was earlier led to believe.

Nobody wants to winter goats and feed them in the cold months unless they are serious about goats and have the numbers to justify the trouble and expense. If you only have 50 or so, the money made is probably not worth the getting up early to feed before you go to your real job. If you have several hundred and this is your real job, then you will want to feed them to the point where they have good finish on them; less than a fat steer, but smooth across the rump. You will also want to market them after most backyard goat producers are out of goats to sell for the year.

You need to have them ready when the market is the highest. This cannot be done if you wean a 60 lb. kid in August,

You need to have them ready when the market is the highest. This cannot be done if you wean a 60 lb. kid in August, creep feeding it and graining his mom to get maximum growth from the kid. This only works for show stock and it pays big dividends but I can't sell 750 show kids. For this reason, it doesn't bother me if my kids only wean 40 lbs. and grow slowly on pasture until I start graining them about 60–90 days before I plan to market them in Jan. or Feb. I would prefer to sell them in Jan. but the market is usually higher in Feb. March is a wild card and I have seen it lower than Feb. In that case you'd have another 30 days of feed in them and didn't get paid for it. I plan on selling my heaviest kids in Jan. and then feeding the lightest ones until Feb. I don't like to have any around in March because I will start kidding again during the end of that month.

During Jan. and Feb. the goat buyers are not so picky about what they buy. Normally a goat over 60 lbs. will not bring as much per lb. as a goat under 60 lbs. From Oct. – Dec. the optimum weight is 50 -60 lbs. A 60 lb. goat was selling for about $1.75 / lb. in the fall of 2010. That totals $105. But if that goat weighs 75lbs. it might have only brought $1.50 x 75 lbs. paying you $112.50, barely enough to cover your feed cost for the additional 15 lbs. Buyers would really prefer to buy the 60 lb. goat. You want to put all the weight on them you can but not so much that they start docking you in price.

During Jan. and Feb. when meat goats aren't as plentiful, the price for the 60 lb. meat goat was $2.20 in Feb. 2011 bringing $132/hd. But the 75 lb. goat would still bring about the same per lb. so it brought $156/hd. Buyers are really in need of goats and don't discount heavier goats if they are good quality. Therefore, by feeding your goats for the Jan. / Feb. market you could gross about $50/hd. more in

> *Therefore, by feeding your goats for the Jan. / Feb. market you could gross about $50/hd. more in some cases.*

some cases. You must be willing to fight with the weather for a couple more months.

I have found that my goats and most everybody's goats that I know need some grain to get the finish on them to become grade #1 meat goats. The amount of grain will depend mostly on the body type or breed of goat that you are feeding. Of course Boer goats will finish out quicker on less feed than a Kiko goat. But with my experience, the Kiko will be the better mother and have less parasite problems than the Boers I have had. There is a cost in having that better Kiko or Spanish mother. Her kids may cost slightly more to feed.

Using a Boer or Myotonic buck would be a good fit. I like a Myotonic X Boer buck, commonly called a TexMaster, on my Spanish and Kiko type does.

These kids weighing 35 lbs. – 45 lbs. at weaning will be grown on pasture, back grounded until Nov. when I begin feeding them more of a grain ration. They'll eat 3% - 4% of their body weight in dry matter, so from about August 15th–November 15th that will be mostly pasture grass or hay for 90 days, probably averaging less than 1.5 lbs. feed intake/hd./day for this time period. Using that figure he would eat about 100 lbs. of grass or hay and you may be feeding him about 50 lbs. of commercial feed over this time. Using $50/ton hay cost, it would take $5.00/hd. for hay or pasture cost and $300/ton feed would make another $6.75 to get him from weaning in mid-August to mid-November when the grain-feeding program begins.

Of course death loss will have to be factored in. During this period you will lose those "Dinky Dinks" that I told you to get rid of earlier. By this time you have vaccinated them and boostered them with CDT and Pneumonia vaccine and may have to deworm them twice during the feeding period. All this will cost you less than $1.00/hd. During this time he may not gain a lot of weight depending on the quality of forage he's eating. We'll say he's gained a little less than .2 lbs./hd./day, so now he weighs 50 - 55 lbs. and it is sometime in November.

Let's look at what post-weaning costs are in this kid up to mid-November:

90 days hay or pasture...................$5.00
90 days commercial feed.................$6.75
Vaccinations and deworming............$1.00
Total.......................................$12.75

Now starts the more intense grain feeding phase. He probably won't be fat enough to be considered a #1 goat unless he is a Pygmy, or maybe some Boer types. If he is fat, he may be worth $1.65/lb. in Nov. according to 2011 prices. If he is still a feeder goat he will probably only bring $1.40/lb. or maybe less. So now he's worth $70 - $75.

For this example let's assume the feeder kid will consume an average of 2 lb./hd./day of the pelleted feed during the feeding period that is now costing $300/ton. He may eat a little less if there is free choice hay but the more of the higher protein feed he eats the more he gains. He should be consuming more than 2 lb./hd./day by the time he is finished. You may need to limit his forage intake to get him up to this amount. If you see him with diarrhea, you will need to back off the grain and increase forage. You will be feeding him for 60 more days; the 120 lbs. of feed will cost you about $18. He will also be eating about .5 lbs. of hay/day, so we will add $2 for that. So now you have another $20 feed cost in the goat.

> *You are never guaranteed a profit, that is the way this business goes, just as with cattle, but you have to be in the game to get a chance to win.*

Let's look at the total cost plus the value of the goat in the August market. Plus the cost of any death loss you have suffered, understanding that half of those were "dinks" who are not worth much anyway. Also, interest on your money should be factored in.

August value of 40 lb. feeder goat.....40 x 1.50 = $60
Feed to Nov.15.......................................$12.75
Vaccine and worming................................. $1.00
Feed to Jan. 15....................................... $20.00
Death loss 5%.......................................$3.00
Interest on money.....................................$3.00
Cost in meat goat by Jan. 15........................ $99.75

This goat should weigh 70 - 75 lbs. and was selling for over $2.00/lb. in Jan. 2011 and 2012 grossing $150.

So for a little less than $40, $99.75 - $60.00, and by fattening the meat goat for the Jan. market, you have increased his value by about $90 netting you about an extra $50/hd.

You are never guaranteed a profit, that is the way this business goes, just as with cattle, but you have to be in the game to get a chance to win.

There are some questions you should ask yourself before feeding these goats out for the higher Jan. / Feb. market.

Do I have the management skill required to handle these kids? If you have been in the cattle business and your practice is to wean and background your own cattle or other calves you buy, then I would say you would get along well with growing goats. You may have a learning curve the first year or two but that is the way with any new venture. If you have limited experience in handling weaned and stressed livestock then the learning curve will be much steeper and probably more costly. You will probably only want to do this on a limited basis starting out — maybe selling most of your kids at weaning and feeding a few to get your feet wet, realizing that things don't always work out in real life as they do on paper. Things happen to goats.

Look at it this way. How long did it take you to become proficient at your current job? If you are currently a car salesman, would you be able to buy a few tools and start building houses for people if you had no experience in construction? How long would it take you to learn the trade and make a profit in a competitive industry? Goats are no different. Raising and growing goats is "skart", half an art and the other half skill. You must learn the skill and perfect the art. It takes a while, you will get discouraged and you will need perseverance to stay at it to gain the experience you need to become successful.

> *Raising and growing goats is "skart", half an art and the other half skill. You must learn the skill and perfect the art.*

Do you have the logistics to handle and feed all the kids you will keep for several months? Do you have storage or handling facilities for their feed? For every 100 kids you feed you will be handling over 200 lbs. of feed every day during some of this feeding period.

Will the market always be higher in Jan. / Feb. than it is in August? It has been the trend over the 10 years that I have been involved with it. Will feeder goats always sell for less per lb. than finished goats? I would assume as this market matures and more people start buying the feeder goats that will change. There are already instances of that trend showing up during some sales. I would expect with more interest in goats and more people in the market for feeder goats the price for them will go up.

I also have some advice for those of you who would consider going into the business of buying and feeding feeder goats. I knew some people that were doing that. Rule number one, you should buy the goats yourself verses using an order buyer. Rule number two, be ready to experience some terrific death losses on occasion. I would only recommend this for those who have been in the business of buying and backgrounding cattle. You must be able to spot a sick goat before he spots you. They have the ability to eat and act almost normal and be dead in 5 minutes. I believe it is a defense mechanism that they know they are prey, and they know predators take the weak and sick as they are easier prey.

> *You must be able to spot a sick goat before he spots you.*

I don't currently buy feeder goats to feed. I've had less trouble and death loss since I quite buying nannies to increase our herd and now only keep our own. I don't want to risk the health of our doe herd by constantly bringing in sale barn feeder goats. If I had another place to keep feeder goats and liked going to sales I might buy some and try it. But I don't and I hate going to sales. I sit there and think about what I need to be doing at home.

CHAPTER 11

WHERE DO YOU SELL YOUR MARKET GOATS?

Meat goats are very easy to market. I have sold at auction barns that have specific goat sales. In my area these sales are usually once a month and are held in the evenings. There are three sales within 90 minutes of where I live. You can check their market reports on the internet.

I have also sold to a buyer who came to the farm and picked up all my meat goats. I liked doing that, as the commission to sell a goat at the sale barn is about $4.00/hd. and maybe another $2.00/hd. in trucking if I have to hire a bigger truck and trailer. But how do you find a buyer? Go to goat sales, as you should do anyway, a few months before your goats are ready, or when you are just getting into the business. Watch who is buying the types of goats you will have for sale and when he's not busy, ask him if he would like to buy goats off of the farm. He will want to know what kind of goats and how many, so he'll know if it is worth his time, because he may be at a sale every day of the week. I have had the most success selling off the farm during the Christmas to New Year's week. Many sales are canceled during this time and if they can get goats from you to send to the packers back East, it keeps their plants open. You may have to take a little less money. or maybe not, depending on how things go. The buyer would weigh his truck and trailer at a grain elevator scale in a nearby town and then come out and load. Then weigh back and write you a check.

A couple words of caution. Once he has agreed to come look at your goats, you should ask other goat producers about him. Make sure he is reputable and has been coming to auction barns for quite a while. If he has, he has a reputation to maintain and will have to be trustworthy in order to stay in business. I would meet him at the scales and verify the empty weight then drive him out to your place. You might take .10 - .15 cents/lb. less than the goat auctions are quoting and still make more money because in a matter of one or two hours you have all your goats gone, you don't have to go to the sale, or haul them or pay commission. He may want to hold back some of the smaller goats, then you have to deal with those, or he may take them all for one price.

My experience with selling at some auction markets is that you may take 100 goats. They run in 50 that look pretty good and bring about the price you expected. Then they run in 25 and bring less money. Then they cut out 15 and bring even less. The last 10 they cut into 2 or 3 groups that don't look so good and don't bring near what you had planned on. When you get your check you're disappointed because the total dollars is several hundred less than what you planned on. Then take off the commission and other selling charges. If you divide that price by the total pounds of goats you sold to get your overall price/lb., you will know what price you would have needed off the farm. Use that as a benchmark for next year's pricing.

There is a goat sale that is about an hour from my house. They have a bad habit of cutting a large group of goats into small groups to run through the sale ring. I recently took a load of 70 market kids to their sale to test the market. They all weighed within 5 lbs.

of each other. I asked the sale manager to not cut them into small bunches, but he let that happen anyway. One buyer was running the cutting gate at the sale and bidding on them. It happened just as I said in the last paragraph. After discussing it with him I told him I couldn't afford to bring him any more goats.

That being said, last year I took 250 market goats to the St. Joseph, Mo., stockyards. I like the fact that there are several buyers there that buy butcher goats and without auction markets there would be no price discovery. The manager, Shane Deering, cut those goats into 2 groups. One group of 175 head, that weighed 68 lbs. and brought $2.02 / lb., and one group of 75 head that weighed 51 lbs. and brought 2.04 / lb. This is one of the ways that a sale barn can work for the livestock producer. You can hide a lot of imperfections in a larger group of goats. This year I took my kids to the St. Joseph stockyards again and was very pleased with the way Shane sorted and showed them in the ring and the price they brought This is just one thing you should watch for as you look for a stockyard to sell your goats for you. At an auction you will get the true

> *At an auction you will get the true worth of your goat, with several buyers there bidding and competing at one time to fill orders for that week.*

worth of your goat, with several buyers there bidding and competing at one time to fill orders for that week. You also walk out with a check in your hands that you know is good.

I suggest getting scales that you can put in your working alley and weigh your meat kids before you sell or even talk to a buyer or sale barn owner. Then you know what to say when he asks, "what do they weigh?" You know what to expect when they go over the scales at the sale. You can also cut out any smaller ones you want to continue to feed. Doing so will make your total bunch look better to a buyer and you should get closer to your asking price.

Some people ask if I sell individual goats off the farm for ethnic holidays, etc. I have done that, but now when someone wants to come by and buy a goat, I usually decline the offer. For me that is a good way to waste half a day. They usually want just one or two goats and want to look at all the goats you have to pick from. If they do show up on time it still takes one or two hours for them to get two goats and for me to get back to doing what I had planned on before they called. I rarely get much more than I would have received at the sale — certainly not enough to justify the trouble.

CHAPTER 12

ENJOY THE CHALLENGE

Now you may be wondering why I raise goats since they are more work and trouble than they appear to be at first glance. You may even be wondering why you ever thought you might want to raise pasture meat goats. Goats are more work than cattle. Death loss is greater in goats than cattle — mostly from parasites and predators. Then there are the fencing issues.

All these obstacles can be overcome, at least to some degree, as I have talked about in the pages of this book. But they will also be overcome when you have set your mind to do it and be successful no matter what it takes. You will find ways of doing things and solving problems that I or no one else would ever dream of. At the end of the day, that's what makes the effort worth it.

There will be times when you are overwhelmed with does kidding or pastures drying up in a drought or a group of does that

> *Just keep working at it, learning new techniques in problem solving until you've worked through that situation.*

seem to keep getting out. Just keep working at it, learning new techniques in problem solving until you've worked through that situation.

Starting anything worthwhile is like turning a flywheel on an engine. At first it takes all that the engine is capable of just to start the flywheel turning. As it turns, the flywheel gains momentum. The flywheel actually helps turn the motor. As the motor goes faster so does the flywheel and the energy expelled by the motor becomes less in proportion to the amount of work it is putting out because of the momentum it has gathered.

It will take time to gather momentum in the goat business — or any business for that matter. As you keep back more doelings and they become productive and produce more doelings, and as you learn new and better ways to be more efficient in the whole production cycle, the flywheel will gain momentum and the energy you expand will decrease as your production increases. This is the way any new business is and especially one about which relatively few people are familiar. You won't have a lot of people to whom you can turn to for help or to gain experience. But you also won't have much competition.

You're somewhat of a pioneer standing alone, looking over a vast expanse of prairie, either seeing the rivers, forest and mountains looming on the horizon and retreating back to civilization, or seeing the opportunity. Most people will turn back and they will encourage others to turn back also because then they won't feel so bad about not going forward. I've had several people tell me they wanted to get into goats, "in a big way." Most of them I never hear from again unless they call to see if I want to buy any of their goats or guardian dogs because they are selling out. Raising goats certainly isn't a cakewalk but neither is any endeavor if you're going to be successful.

Raising meat goats is an untapped resource in most areas of the U.S., especially from the Midwest to the East Coast. You already may have pasture where brush and weeds are a constant battle to control but where meat goats would thrive. In that case you wouldn't need to change your stocking rate on your cattle at all. Simply add goats that would eat what the cattle aren't eating or what you are mowing off every year. That's the essence of making lemonade out of the lemons you've been battling.

Raising meat goats is an untapped resource in most areas of the U.S., especially from the Midwest to the East Coast.

You may be able to find pasture that is unsuitable for cattle or on which someone else has cattle grazing that would want to control their brush. I have several meat goats with other people's cattle that are eating their brush and weeds. Subsequently, there is usually goat pasture available in the area where you live, when more cattle pasture is hard to lease. You can probably drive around in a few miles from your home and find pasture that the operator has to mow every year or it would be taken over by tree sprouts or cedar trees, or maybe it already has been and would make excellent goat pasture. Some brushy pastures get abandoned because nobody wants to rent them or the fences are not worth fixing. You will need to run electric wire anyway so you may make a deal with the current owner of the property to lease it for a few years for free to see what the goats will do for it. If you are a cattle producer you probably have this kind of pasture yourself. All in all, goat pasture is easier to find than cattle pasture in the Midwestern United States.

I don't believe I have ever aggressively sought out goat pasture. Many times I have been ask by cattle operators to bring my goats to control their weeds and brush.

> *goat pasture is easier to find than cattle pasture in the Midwestern United States.*

You may have sons or daughters that want to become part of your farm or ranching operation. This is a way they can work their way into the business if you don't have any extra land resources for them. Give them some goat-type pastures with fences that won't hold cattle anymore. Or you may be able to hire a full-time employee that would handle the meat goats and help you with other ranch or farm work that needs done, the goats paying his wages.

Sometimes I think goats are easier to handle than cattle and that may be true, depending on how you handle them. A goat in a pasture with a sore foot is easier to catch and doctor than a cow with the same problem. But sometimes I find myself straining to lift, push or carry goats, because I can, when I would never try to do that with cattle. If you are not physically able to handle cattle, goats would be another option that may work better for you.

The profitability for goats is similar to cattle. If you average selling one kid per doe for $2.00 - $2.50 / lb. and calves sell for $1.50 - $1.75 / lb. the extra $.50 - $.60 / lb. should offset the extra expense and problems that arise with goats, once you are able to manage those problems more easily and economically. If you can get your average kid crop up to 1.3 or more kids sold per doe every year, then they can be more profitable than cattle, though they are extra work.

You may feel discouraged because I have emphasized the problems I've encountered as I've been raising Pasture Meat Goats.

That is the purpose of this book: To help you understand what you're getting into. I would not be fair to you if I only told you about the enjoyment involved with being a Pasture Meat Goat Producer.

It would not be fair of me to only tell you of the pleasure you'll have in going out on a warm spring evening and seeing a mob of kids a few weeks old, running together like a swarm of bees, jumping and bucking as if to say, "Catch me if you can!"

Or the feeling of accomplishment you'll get from taking what most would consider a worthless brushy pasture and cleaning it of brush and weeds while making an income off of it. Or the feeling of success you'll receive when you see your herd growing and becoming more easily managed. You will know and understand things about goats and guardian dogs that very few people will ever know. You will be able to take a pasture that is an eyesore and has little economic value and use it to produce a viable income, while watching it look more like a city park. You will be a leader in a growing and prosperous industry, ready to take advantage of opportunities as they appear.

> *You will be a leader in a growing and prosperous industry, ready to take advantage of opportunities as they appear.*

Due to the large influx of other cultures moving into America, and those people being very prosperous, the meat goat demand is growing every year with no sign of it slowing. To eat goat meat is part of their culture, just as grilling a steak on a cool summer evening is part of the culture of the Midwestern U.S. There will continue to be a high demand for your product.

Everything points to the Eastern half of the U. S. as an area where the meat goat population is going to expand exponentially as pasture goats become more easily managed. You can see the growth in recent years by looking at the number of goat sales that take place every month and the amount of goats that go through those auctions.

If you have become discouraged and overwhelmed by what you have read here and decide not to venture into the meat goat business, then this book will have saved you thousands of dollars. If you've read this and believe goats are a good fit for you and your resources, then this book will be worth even more.

If you've read this book and honestly don't think it is worth the purchase price, you can contact me through my website at www.grandviewlivestock.com, and I will personally send your money back.

You can also contact me to ask other questions or simply talk goats.

EPILOGUE

I wrote this closing poem during a summer of drought and other misfortunes to encourage myself. I hope it does the same for you, if not, it's no extra charge.

Dare to Win

I'll call diamonds, he said with a grin;
As he sat his drink back down.
My pile in front was smaller now,
As he won another round.

It'd been that way for o'er an hour
As he rarely lost a bid.
"The cards are hot for you tonight".
In reply the stranger said,

You wanna win the game at hand?
Then the bid ya have to take.
There's times it'll bust ya flat
But most the time you'll make.

You'll find a way down deep inside
That you didn't know you had.
You'll think you can't, but when you do,
It was really not so bad.

You'll find new ways of winning,
When your backs against the wall.
That you never would've found,
If the cards, you'd just let fall.

If what's in your hand is all you see,
You'll probably not go far.
You always need be countin',
The cards you're gonna draw.

Life's a risk ya gotta take,
Or, it's just a way of dying.
If you never step off the cliff,
You'll not know the joy of flying.

Greg Christiansen

ACKNOWLEDGEMENTS

As I was finishing this book and having others read through it, I was asked, "what made you want to write a book anyway?"

If I am honest with myself and nobody was listening, I would probably say, "I wanted to see my name on the cover of a book" or "I want to be seen as an expert in something" or "I wanted to fulfill a lifelong dream" or "I want people to think more of me than I really am" or "that I want to be recognized and held in esteem by my peers." Notice how the truth begins with "I". These are all very selfish and conceited reasons but are probably the true reasons we do most everything we do. I say "we" because I am just an average guy. Such is human nature.

But to your face, if you ask me why I wanted to write a book, I would say, "I believe everyone lives his life with at least one good book inside them. After a few years in any career, be it construction worker, banker, school teacher or medical doctor, all of us have learned much about our profession that would help and encourage those just entering into it or struggling along the way. When we were beginning our career there was so much we did not know that we didn't know what questions to ask. It is so good to have someone to come beside you that has walked that way before and stumbled upon the same rocky path but got up and kept going, smoothing the road out as they moved on and marking the path for you to follow." I would not be lying when I told you that either.

Interesting how God will use even our selfish, self-centered motives to help and encourage others. As I get to know Him better, I find that He's kind of sneaky that way.

Many times we don't see those that smoothed the road out before us until we look backward. Now I would like to look back down the road and thank those who helped move the obstacles that you never see as you begin.

I would begin by thanking my family.

My wife Ann, who only occasionally questioned my sanity in keeping the meat goat business alive and growing as we struggled through various problems and disappointments, like keeping more replacement doelings instead of selling them as meat goat kids, which cut into our paycheck. She has had goats in her house, in her kitchen sink, lying next to the wood stove, and listened to them bawl at night sounding like they were in bed with us. She has bottle fed as many as 10 kids at once and suffered disappointment when things didn't work out as planned. She has done without things she could have had so we could buy goat feed or supplies with only a hope and a prayer that we would get a return on our investment above the interest that we were paying the bank.

My two daughters, Ashley and Megan, who spent hours during their teenage years grabbing and vaccinating goats, writing numbers down and filling syringes when they would have rather been doing things that other teenage girls were doing but never refused to help when I needed them

My son Tanner Wade, who borrowed money and bought backyard goats with his father, and then struggled to pay back the loan with his "goat check" that often wasn't as much as our cash flow statement said it should be He has stood on the front lines with me during all the trials we've encountered over the years, taking the full brunt of my emotions that I will not explain but if you have livestock you will definitely understand, and if you help someone else with livestock you will know why I feel the need to apologize for all things said and done while handling them. It has been a dream come true to work and be in business with my son. We have gotten to know each other in ways very few fathers get to know their teenage sons.

Sweating it out with your family by you makes it all worth it.

I would like to thank Duff Sandness. We cut our teeth in the goat business together, learning from each other's experience. I'm sure I gained more than I gave. I often miss the trips we took as far as South Texas to buy goats and learn from workshops and other producers. Not to mention the good Border Collies I got from Duff and the teaching I received on how to train them. I'm sure I would have given up without you as a sounding board, as you could well understand the problems encountered.

I received wisdom from Dr. David Sparks DVM, Area Food-Animal Quality and Health Specialist, OSU Cooperative Extension Service, and Dr. Steve Hart, Goat Extension Specialist, Langston University, Langston, Okla., during goat seminars and FAMACHA training. They both team together along with other colleagues, putting on goat seminars that are well worth the time of any goat producer. These men independently proofread my original manuscript, gracefully offering wisdom and ideas with their suggestions in areas ranging from goat care to grammar that only scholars can give. Their personal reviews gave me encouragement and energy to move forward after the task of writing this book ceased to be fun and exciting and was more like work.

I am grateful for the friendship of Michael Hogan, Rob Wood and Jack Pisano, fellow goat ranchers that I confer with often and who kept my feet to the fire and took the time to read the early manuscripts. I would like to thank them for any ideas I stole from them and have put in print here. They offered experience from another pasture goat rancher's perspective and allowed me to gauge the readability of the manuscript.

I am very appreciative of Terry Hankins, publisher and editor of *Goat Rancher* magazine and a goat rancher himself for many years, for doing the final editing of this book. He may be the only person alive with experience in these two fields and I am very fortunate to have his skill involved in the final stages of this project.

Please do not hold any of these fine people accountable for the contents of this book or blame them if you feel mislead by something I put in print. Although, I feel that all of these men are experts in the field of raising goats and could have written a more comprehensive book on the subject, I am solely responsible for the content here and I have tried my best to be honest and forthright in relaying only my own experiences, therefore giving me the right to respectfully ask you, the reader, for your time and money. I have included their contact information in the back of this book that you should keep as a resource; I ask only that you would be respectful of their time.

I would also like to thank you, the reader, for taking the time to read, and hopefully, perfect the art and hone the skill, "Skart", of raising Meat Goats. There is so much information available on any subject imaginable and I feel privileged you've read this far. I wrote this book to be used, not just read. My hope is that it will be worn from use as you pull it from your shelf when you encounter a rock or pothole in the road of pasture raising Commercial Meat Goats. I desire that you would receive not only practical solutions to problems that arise but also encouragement and confidence that they can be overcome.

Finally I would like to thank my Lord and Creator for all the experiences he has given me that went into the words on these pages. I know he has forgiven me but I would like to apologize again in print for the times I yelled out in disgust because things didn't go as (I) had planned. I've been told that, "Life is lived forward but understood backward," and that is true, but I would add that sometimes it's not understood until it's over, so deal with it.

APPENDIX

Books on my shelf
I have several but these are the only two books I ever use.

Sheep & Goat Medicine by D. G. Pugh

Meat Goat Production Hand Book
This can be purchased through Langston University's website
to order the Meat Goat Production Handbook
http://www.luresext.edu/goats/handbookorderform.pdf

Websites I often use:

Langston University
http://www.luresext.edu/index.htm

Oklahoma State University
www.oklagoats.com

Goat Rancher Magazine
www.goatrancher.com
From this website you can find USDA reported goat sales across
the Midwest, and a lot of other goat related stuff. Good magazine
too.

OTHER MEAT GOAT PRODUCERS AND GOOD CONTACTS:

Michael Hogan
www.w3ranch.com

Rob Wood
http://middlecreekmeatgoats.webs.com

Jack Pisano
(913) 757-3368

Dr. David Sparks DVM
www.goathillkikos.com

Dr. Steve Hart
(405) 466-6138 or at shart@luresext.edu

Terry Hankins
www.egyptcreekranch.com

Fence chargers and fence supplies
www.taylorfence.net
www.kencove.com
www.premier1supplies.com
www.powerflexfence.com

Vet supplies
www.valleyvet.com
www.livestockconcepts.com